LEAP AHE

with

MATHS

Book 6

Brian Nash
Paul Nightingale

Consultant
Brenda Apsley

Illustrated by Jan Wade

NIGHTINGALE PRESS

NIGHTINGALE PRESS
Devised and produced by Nightingale Press
Unit 5b Causeway Park Industrial Estate, Wilderspool Causeway,
Warrington, Cheshire WA4 6QE England

This edition produced in 1995 for Pegasus Distribution Ltd.,
Unit 5b Causeway Park Industrial Estate, Wilderspool Causeway,
Warrington, Cheshire WA4 6QE England

First published in Great Britain in 1995
by Nightingale Press

Editor Consultant: Brenda Apsley
Illustrator: Jan Wade

Printed in Australia

ISBN 1 - 875288 - 74 - 0

About this book

The most effective learning comes as the result of a three-way partnership between parent, child and teacher in a total learning environment which combines home, school and the outside world. Encouragement, together with repeated practice and investigation will develop skills and confidence, enabling children to get ahead in maths.

The seven books in the series have a revision overlap; thus, the first five units of this book revise and reinforce work covered in Book 5.

Each activity and task is designed to be 'self guiding', but you should offer help when it is needed, explaining concepts and terminolgy. Children should not require close supervision.

Look for opportunities to practise maths. Talk about prices in supermarkets and restaurants, and discuss what discount offers mean. Talk about motorway distance signs and encourage children to become familiar with bus and train timetables and flight times. We are surrounded by maths, so the opportunities are endless!

Key words in maths are printed in **bold** type. Answers are given in the middle of the book, but do not over-emphasise the importance of being 'right' every time. The main objective is in building confidence and understanding.

1.
```
  5 1
  1 7
+   8
-----
```

2.
```
  2 7
  3 8
+ 1 6
-----
```

3.
```
  4 6
  3 5
+ 1 8
-----
```

4.
```
  3 7
  2 9
+   6
-----
```

Fill in the missing numbers.

5.
```
  2 5
  ___
+ 2 2
-----
  7 7
```

6.
```
  3 _
  1 5
+ _ 8
-----
  8 5
```

7.
```
  6 _
  2 7
+ 3 9
-----
  _ 8
```

8.
```
  1 1
  _ 7
+ 3 _
-----
  9 3
```

9. 24 + 33 + 12 + 9 = ______

10. 18 + 7 + 54 + 11 = ______

11. 20 + 34 + 4 + 17 = ______

12. 11 + 22 + 33 + 44 = ______

13. Finish the **addition** square. **Add** numbers in the top row to those down the side. One is done.

+	19	32	14	25
17	**36**			
29				
11				
37				

14. 68 - 29 = ______

15. 50 - 37 = ______

16. 77 - 48 = ______

17. 83 - 46 = ______

18. Sam caught **35** tadpoles one day and **23** the next. He gave away **19.** How many left? ______

19. Penny had **44** stamps. She swapped **17** for **22.** How many stamps did she finally have? ______

20. **54** marbles **minus 17.** How many left? ______

21. Name each **3-D** shape. Colour the **prisms.**

(a) 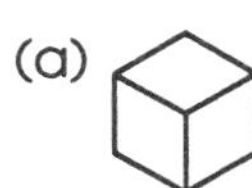

(b)

(c)

______ ______ ______

(d) 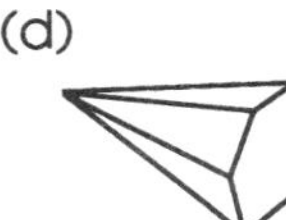

(e) 

(f) 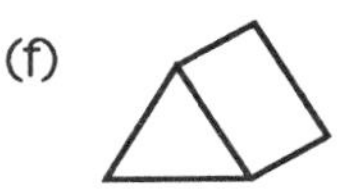

______ ______ ______

22. Draw two other arrangements of these twelve blocks.

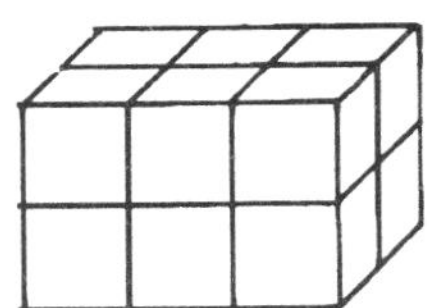

23. Draw a different view of each object. Label the view **below, top, side,** or **back.**

(a) 

(b) 

(c) 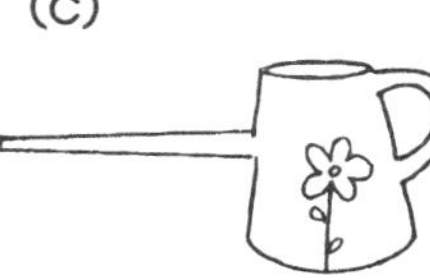

1. Measure and record the **area** of each shape in **square centimetres (cm²)**.

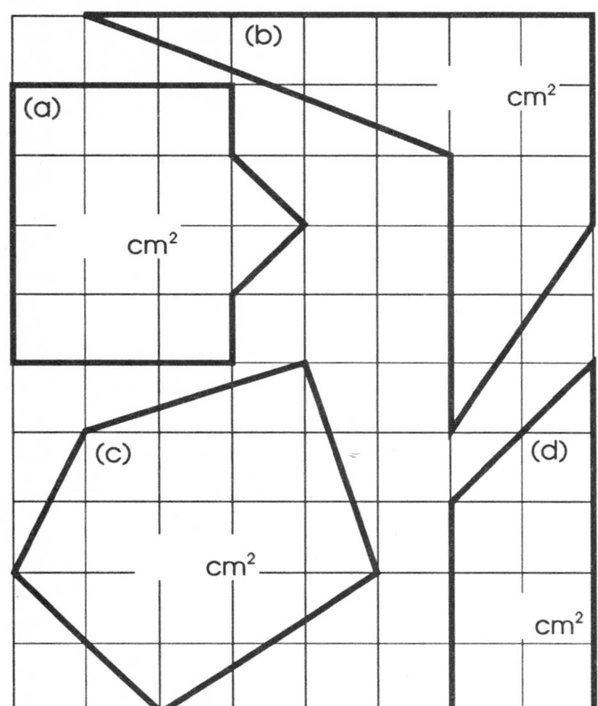

2. Colour the shape that has the **larger** area, then measure and record each **area** in **square centimetres (cm²)**.

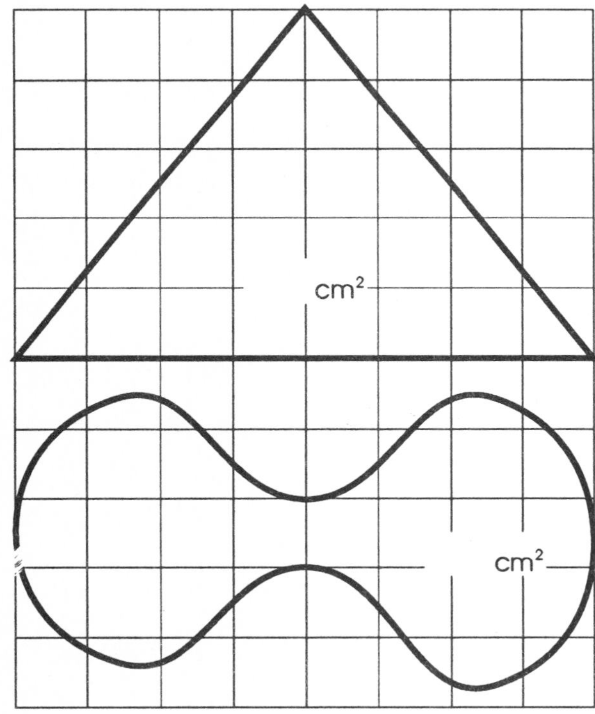

3. Draw the **top view** of each object.

(a) (b) (c)

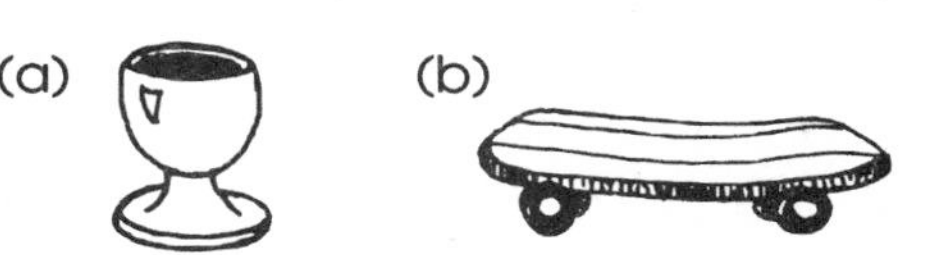

4. 88 - 35 = ______
5. 35 - 16 = ______
6. 94 - 47 = ______
7. 86 - 58 = ______
8. 74 - 55 = ______
9. 81 - 29 = ______

10. Make two different objects from 7 **cubes** and draw them here.

11. Draw a **rectangular prism.**

12. 21 + 43 + 11 + 7 = ______
13. 49 + 22 + 15 + 27 = ______
14. 67 + 18 + 34 + 9 = ______
15. 34 + 8 + 17 + 7 + 25 = ______

16. Complete the addition table.

+	27	43	61	39	54	66	25
21							

17.
```
  37
  16
+ 45
----
```

18.
```
  14
   8
+ 56
----
```

19.
```
   9
  14
+ 29
----
```

20.
```
  28
  49
+  6
----
```

1. 58 − 27 = ____

2. 44 − 19 = ____

3. 65 − 37 = ____

4. 76 − 43 = ____

5. 93 − 68 = ____

6. 81 − 27 = ____

7. 62 − 39 = ____

8. 77 − 48 = ____

9. Complete the **subtraction** fan.

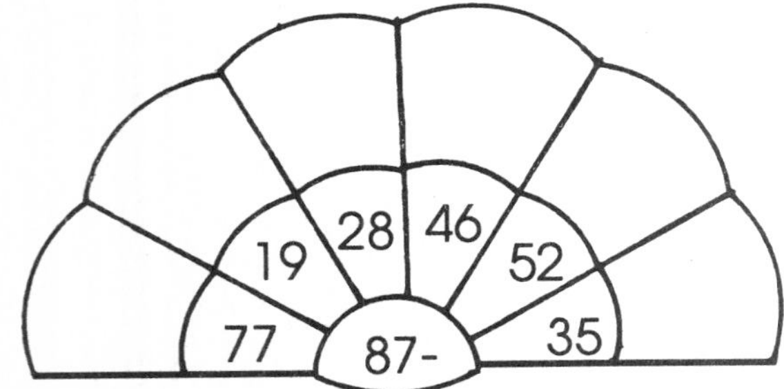

10. 148 x 2 = ____

11. 219 x 3 = ____

12. 175 x 4 = ____

13. 137 x 5 = ____

14. 116 x 6 = ____

15. 94 x 7 = ____

16. Complete the **multiplication** table.

x	216	342	167	89	185
7					

17. A policeman booked **43** drivers every day for **5** days. How many bookings altogether? ____

18. If potatoes are **£4** per bag, how much for **39** bags? £ ____

19. A plane carries **26** passengers each trip. How many in **7** trips? ____

20. **56** rows of **9** seats. How many seats altogether? ____

21. Make these models using strips of card and paper fasteners. Add another stip to make each model rigid.

(a) 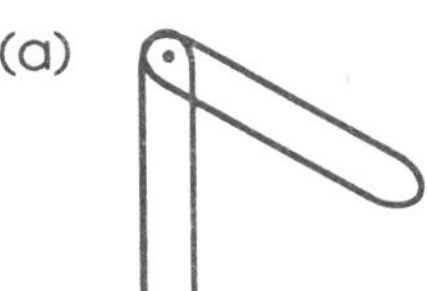

(b) 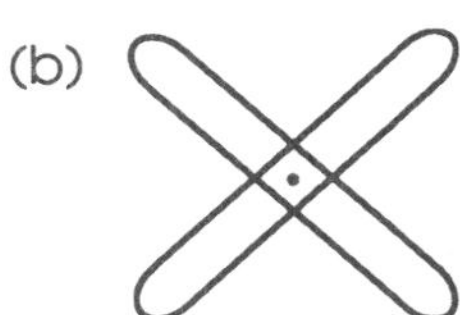

(c) 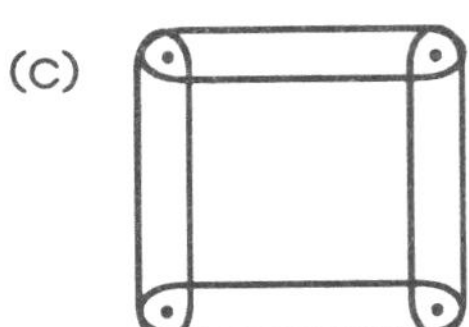

(d) 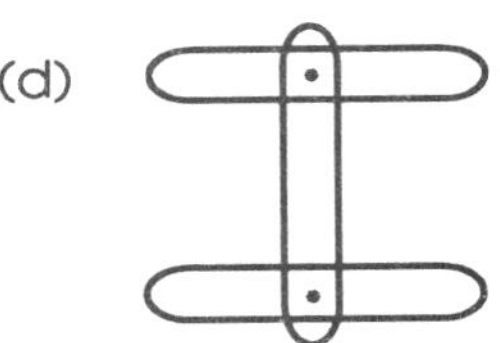

22. Mark where you would cut or fold this triangle to make the shape below.

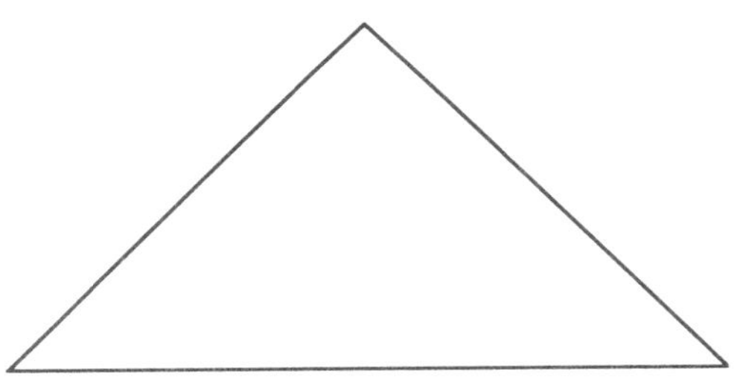

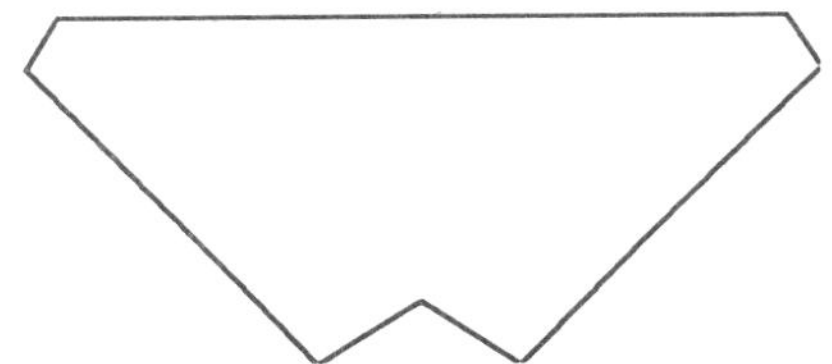

23. Name each **polygon.**

(a) 

____

(b) 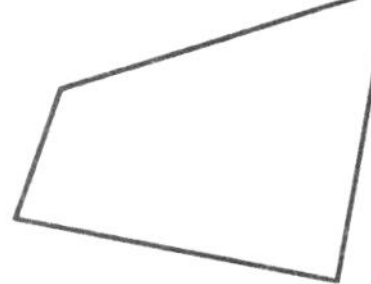

____

(c) 

____

(d) 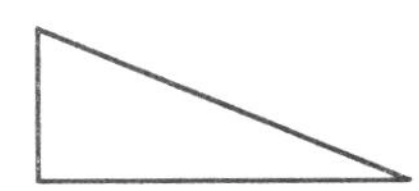

____

1. List **containers** that have **capacities** similar to these.

1l ______

½l ______

250ml ______

200ml ______

150ml ______

Add these **capacities.**

2. 3l 120ml + 2l 300ml = ______
3. 4l 250ml + 3l 750ml = ______
4. 5l 420ml + 2l 630ml = ______
5. 750ml + 2l 425ml = ______
6. 6l 550ml + 15ml = ______

7. Write the unit of **capacity** for each **container.**

(a)  (b)  (c) 

1250 ______ 10 ______ 500 ______

8. Find the **capacity** of a soft drink can. ______

9. What is the **capacity** of a small tetra juice pack? ______

10. Write each **measurement** in short form. The first one is done for you.

(a) 250 millilitres 0.25l or 250ml

(b) 850 millilitres ______

(c) 2 360 millilitres ______

(d) 6 millilitres ______

11.	12.	13.	14.
54	76	81	97
-25	-39	-36	-68
______	______	______	______

15. 123- 5= ______
16. 137- 2= ______
17. 231- 3= ______
18. 186- 4= ______
19. 119- 7= ______
20. 144- 6= ______

Add these **capacities.**

21. 2l 130ml + 1l 420ml = ______
22. 3l 25ml + 2l 110ml = ______
23. 2l 125ml + 3l 125ml = ______
24. 6l 300ml + 3l 700ml = ______
25. 5l 420ml + 2l 150ml = ______

26. Complete the **addition** wheel.

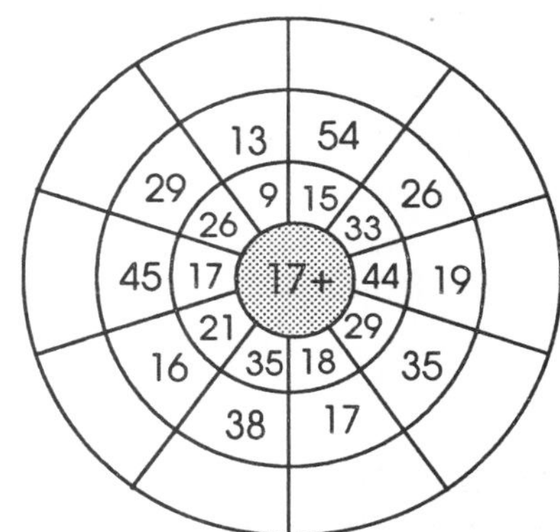

Complete these **subtractions.**

27. 6l - 4l 500ml = ______
28. 5l - 3l 750ml = ______
29. 4l 500ml - 1l 250ml = ______
30. 7l 250ml - 4l 200ml = ______

1. 63 ÷ 9 = ______

2. 56 ÷ 7 = ______

3. 28 ÷ 4 = ______

4. 48 ÷ 8 = ______

5. 35 ÷ 5 = ______

6. 54 ÷ 6 = ______

7. 80 ÷ 10 = ______

8. 45 ÷ 9 = ______

9. 72 ÷ 8 = ______

10. 72 ÷ 6 = ______

Write these **fractions** in **decimal** form. The first one is done.

11. two tenths 0.2

12. eight tenths ________

13. thirty-four tenths ________

14. sixteen tenths ________

15. twenty-seven tenths ________

16. Complete the **division** wheel.

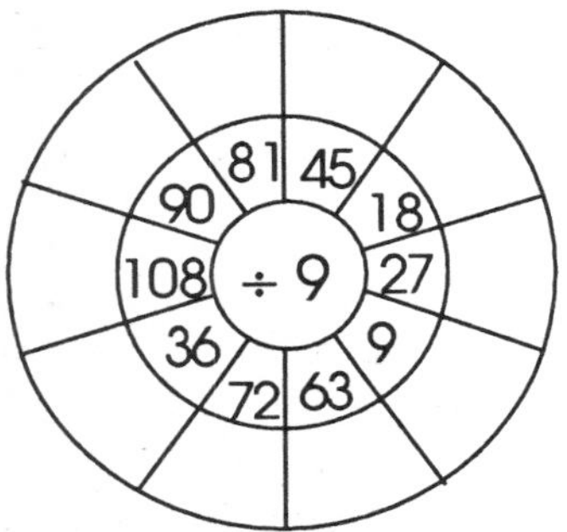

Show these **hundredths** on the grids.

17. 0.3

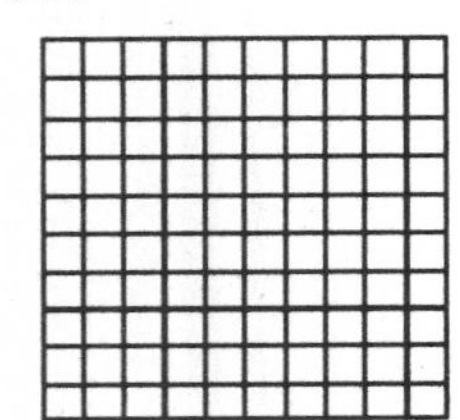

18. 0.75

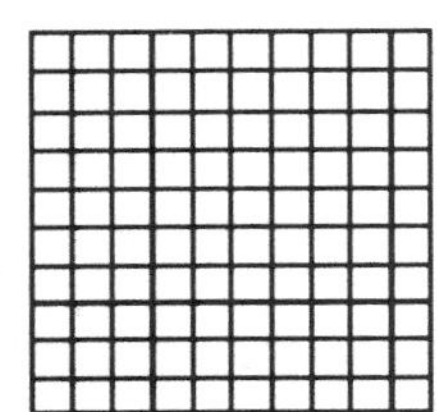

19. 0.46

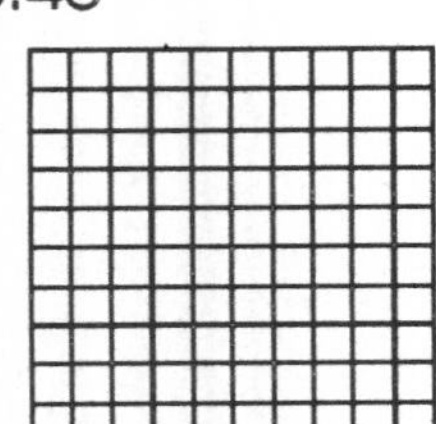

20. 0.9

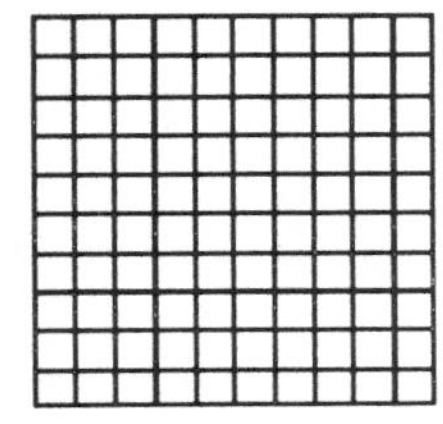

21. Find the Pharaoh's treasure by drawing the correct **path** through the **maze.**

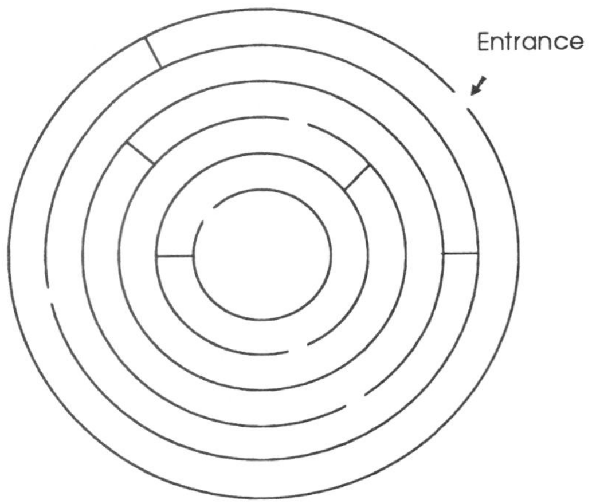

This graph shows average desert **temperatures** for seven months.

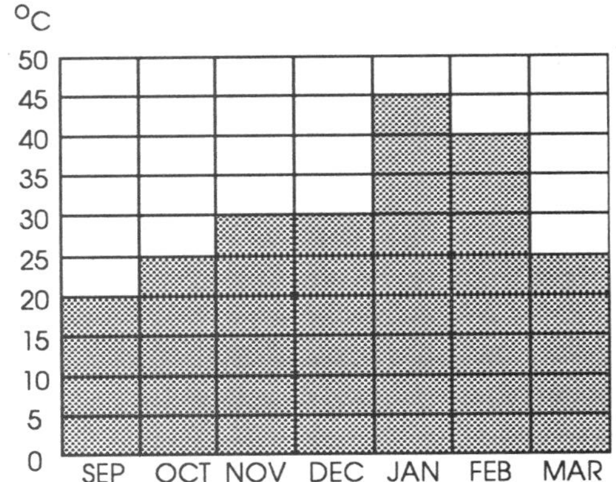

22. What is the **highest temperature** on the graph? ______

23. What is the lowest **temperature?** ______

24. In what month was the lowest **temperature** recorded? ______

25. What is the difference between the highest and lowest **temperature?** ______

26. What is the **temperature** range for each division on the **graph?** ______

27. If the June **temperature** is **30°C** less than the highest on the graph, what is the June **temperature?** ______

28. If you had to include a **temperature** for April, what might it be? ______

Find and record the **temperature** for each of the following.

1. In a hot bath ______
2. Inside an air-conditioned building ______
3. At a holiday resort on a hot day ______
4. In a cool-room where fruit or meat is stored ______
5. In a bubbling hot spring ______
6. Read the **temperature.**

______ C°

7. Do you know something that is about this **temperature?**

______

8. Fill in the table.
   (a) 60 seconds = ______
   (b) 60 minutes = ______
   (c) 24 hours = ______
   (d) 7 days = ______
   (e) 52 weeks = ______
   (f) 10 years = ______
   (g) 100 years = ______
9. How many days in one year? ______
10. How many days from 13th October to 10th November? ______
11. Show thirty-seven minutes past nine on the analog and digital clocks.

12. How many days in a lunar month? ______

Write these **fractions** in decimal form.

13. 17 tenths ______
14. 1 tenth ______
15. 6 tenths ______
16. 28 tenths ______
17. 43 tenths ______
18. 10 tenths ______

Write these as **hundredths.**

19. 0.6 ______
20. 2.73 ______
21. 0.85 ______
22. 1.09 ______

27 ÷ 9 = 3

23. 81 ÷ 9 = ______
24. 56 ÷ 8 = ______
25. 60 ÷ 6 = ______
26. 64 ÷ 8 = ______
27. 63 ÷ 7 = ______
28. 72 ÷ 9 = ______
29. How many seconds in five minutes? ______
30. How many hours in three days? ______
31. Write 18 months as years. ______
32. Make up three safety rules for handling a thermometer.
   (a) ______
   (b) ______
   (c) ______

Add five to each number.

1. 23 461 ________
2. 68 703 ________
3. 58 197 ________
4. 40 099 ________
5. 69 999 ________
6. 72 478 ________

Rearrange each group of numbers to make the **smallest** number possible.

7. 19 402 ____________
8. 28 742 ____________
9. 50 614 ____________
10. 47 393 ____________

Write these numbers in expanded form. The first one is done for you.

11. 63 023 60 000 + 3 000 + 000 + 20 + 3
12. 78 427 ________ + ______ + _____ + ____ + ___
13. 7 545 ________ + ______ + _____ + ____
14. 43 091 ________ + ______ + _____ + ____ + ___
15. 91 999 ________ + ______ + _____ + ____ + ___

16. Complete the **subtraction** web.

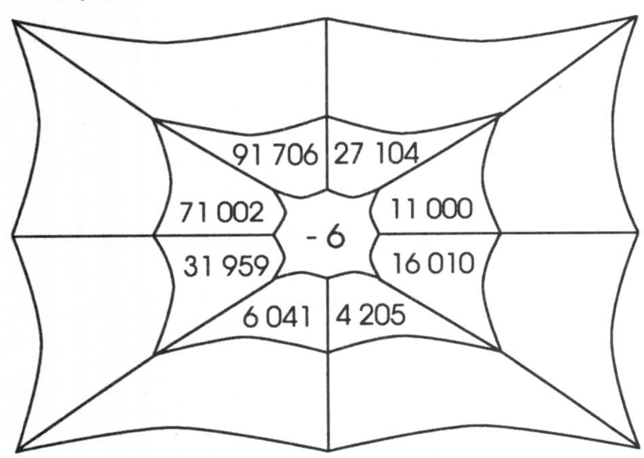

Rearrange each group of numbers to make the **largest** number.

17. 21 768 ____________
18. 54 192 ____________

19. Draw the jug from the top.

top view

20. This is the end view of a toaster. Draw the **front** view.

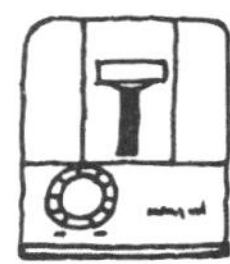

front view

21. This is a rowing boat seen from the side. Draw the **top** view.

top view

22. Draw the **underneath** view of the bell.

underneath view

23. Count the number of cubes and faces visible in each **3-D** object.

(a)

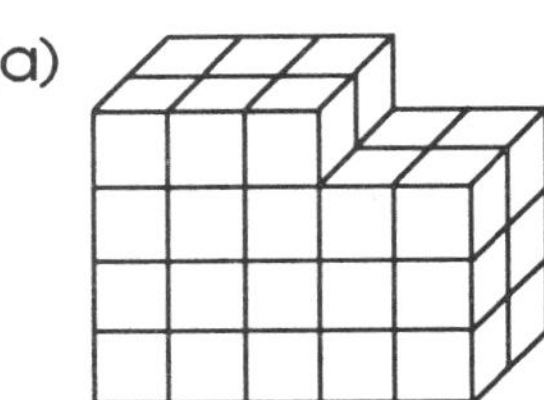

cubes ______

faces ______

(b)

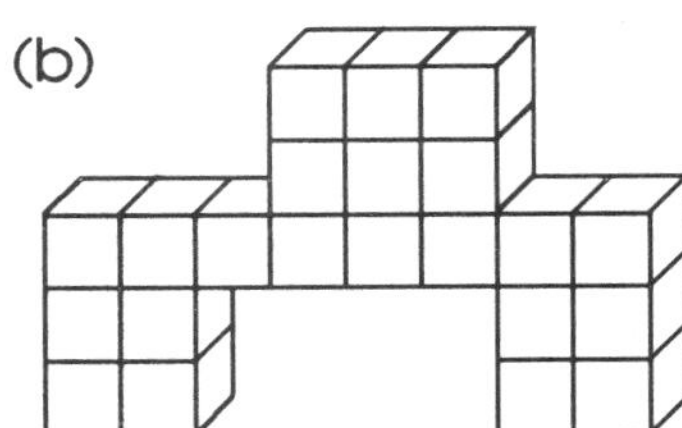

cubes ______

faces ______

(c)

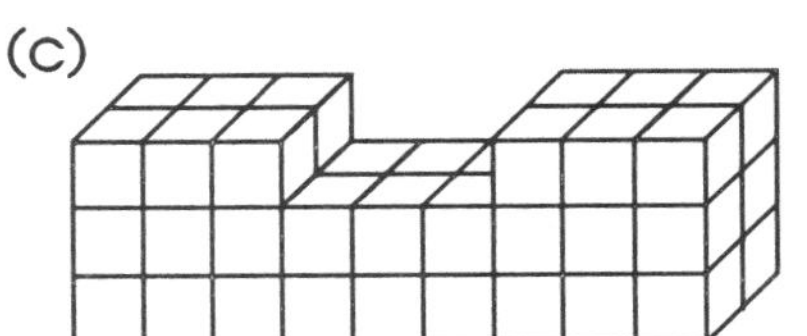

cubes ______

faces ______

1. Write each length in **centimetres (cm)**, then in decimal form as **metres (m)**.

Length	cm	m
1 metre 30 centimetres		
4 metres 56 centimetres		
17 metres 50 centimetres		
3 metres 11 centimetres		
86 metres 15 centimetres		
25 metres 7 centimetres		

2. Open this book right out and measure its **perimeter**. ________

3. Measure the **longest** side of the building you are in. ________

4. Measure the **width** of a garage door. ________

5. Find a big tree and measure around its trunk at ground level. ________

6. How tall are you? ________

7. Use a piece of wool or cotton to measure the **length** of this line.

______ cm

8. Measure these lines to the nearest **centimetre**.

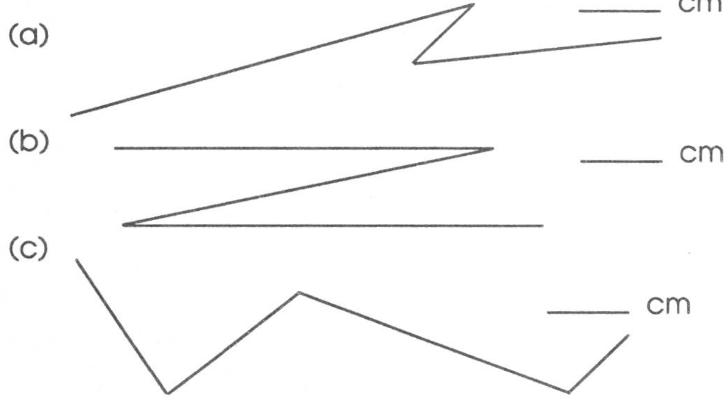

(a) ______ cm

(b) ______ cm

(c) ______ cm

Rearrange the numbers to make the biggest and smallest numbers possible.

	Numbers	Biggest Number	Smallest Number
9.	69 405		
10.	45 871		
11.	36 529		
12.	87 742		
13.	22 384		
14.	17 961		

Write these **expanded** numbers in short form.

15. 40 000 + 2 000 + 700 + 80 + 3 = ______

16. 70 000 + 7 000 + 300 + 40 + 5 = ______

17. 90 000 + 5 000 + 900 + 50 + 9 = ______

18. 9 000 + 800 + 6 = ______

19. How many cubes in this object?

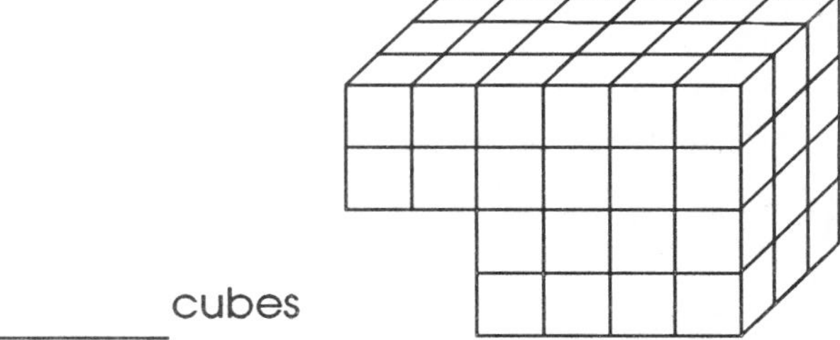

________ cubes

Write these **lengths** in **centimetres (cm)**.

20. 23 metres 32 centimetres ____________

21. 8 metres 57 centimetres ____________

22. 10 metres 49 centimetres ____________

23. Measure these lines in centimetres.

(a)

______ cm

(b)

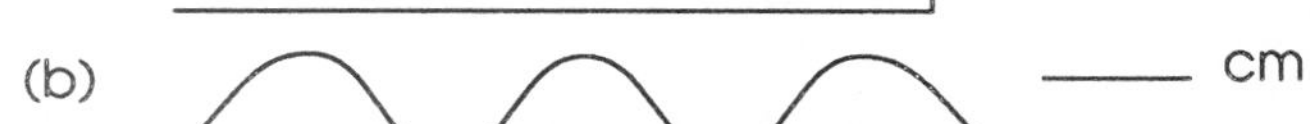

______ cm

Write these words as numbers.

1. Sixty-one thousand eight hundred and seventy-five ________
2. Thirty-two thousand and fifty-one ________
3. Eighty-nine thousand eight hundred and ninety-eight ________
4. Eleven thousand one hundred and one ________
5. Ninety-four thousand four hundred and thirteen ________

Add **1 000** to these numbers, then add another **400** to complete the table.

Number	+ 1 000	+ 400
6. 25 316		
7. 78 348		
8. 73 265		
9. 90 120		
10. 53 125		

Write the **value** of numbers in bold (ten thousands, thousands, hundreds, tens or units).

11. **71** 240 ________________
12. 25 2**5**0 ________________
13. 36 **5**18 ________________
14. **8**1 534 ________________
15. 47 18**9** ________________

16. Write these sets of numbers in order, **smallest** to **largest**.

(a) 66 904   8 942   66 940   9 423

____

(b) 71 521   75 211   72 502   73 201

____

Rearrange these 6 cubes to make three different solids. Draw the **top, front** and **side views** of each solid.

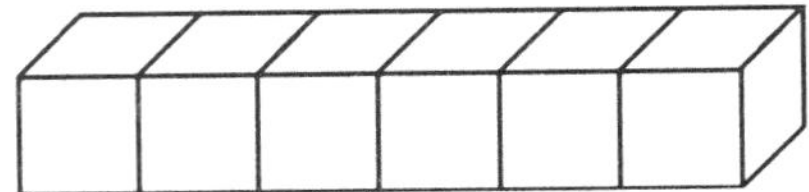

17.

18.

19.

Make **3-D** drawings of these two prisms on the grid.

20. Front View   End View   Top View

21. Front View   End View   Top View

Measure these **areas** in **square centimetres.**

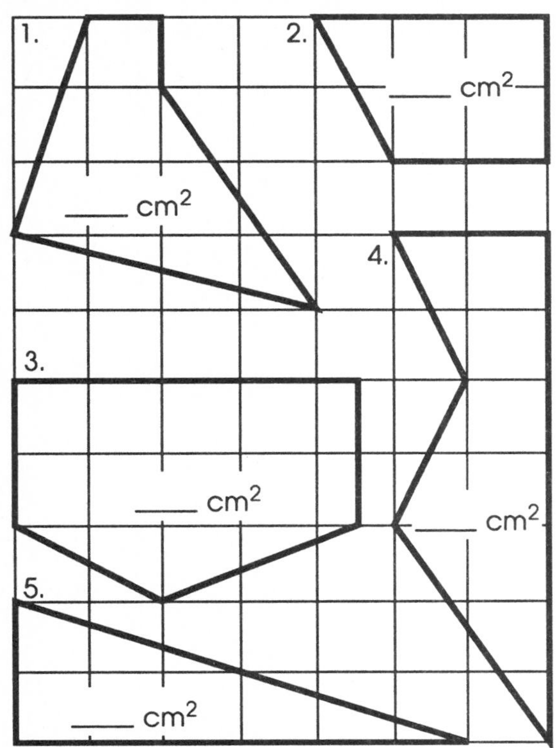

6. Trace around your hand and foot on **one centimetre squared grid** paper. Measure and record the **area** of each.

(a) hand ______ cm² (b) foot ______ cm²

Find the areas.

7. A postage stamp ________
8. A small envelope ________
9. A large envelope ________
10. Sheet of A4 paper ________
11. A newspaper page ________
12. Find the **surface** (total) area of a drink can. ________
13. What is the area of your desk top? ________
14. Find the area of your seat. ________
15. What is the area of a rug or mat? ________

Write these numbers in falling order - largest to smallest.

16. 13 618 9 540 14 861 86 432

____

17. 11 590 15 108 10 794 14 652

____

18. 9 754 7 945 8 976 7 459

____

19. 51 742 48 751 49 642 50 830

____

Write these numbers in words.

20. 14 051 ________________________________

21. 78 923 ________________________________

22. 93 304 ________________________________

Write the **value** of the bold numbers. (ten thousands, thousands, hundreds, tens or units).

23. 72 **1**30 ________ 24. **4** 163 ________

25. 56 14**5** ________ 26. **63** 157 ________

Measure these **areas** in **square centimetres.**

27. A £5 note ____ 28. A credit card ____

29. The base of a calculator ____ 30. A big leaf ____

31. Front of a CD container ____ 32. Base of a telephone ____

33. Find the total **surface area** of this model made of 1cm cubes.

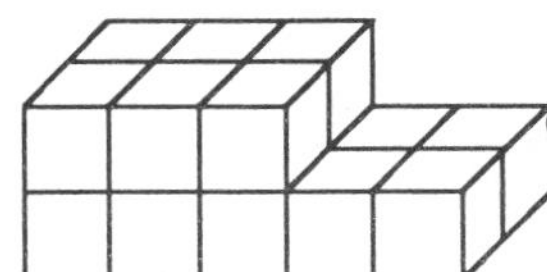

______ cm²

1. 19 + 26 + 33 + 7 = ______

2. 34 + 9 + 17 + 15 = ______

3. 22 + 48 + 11 + 19 = ______

4. 16 + 35 + 27 + 56 = ______

5. 48 + 23 + 21 + 7 = ______

6. Alison went fishing for three days. She caught 28 fish, 16 fish and 33 fish. How many fish did she catch altogether? ______

7. Her big brother Alan caught 38 fish, 25 fish and 17 fish. How many did he catch altogether? ______

8. Four Scouts were collecting 10 pence pieces for a 'kilometre of coins'. The Scouts collected 36 coins, 28 coins, 30 coins and 26 coins. How many altogether? ______

9. What was the value of the 10 pence coins collected by the Scouts in question 8? ______

10.	11.	12.	13.
23	18	35	29
14	37	26	57
+ 48	+ 29	+ 13	+ 36
______	______	______	______

14. Complete the **addition** square.

+	15	3	12	
	8		13	33
	11	6		21
			29	

15. 16 + 9 + 27 - 12 = ______

Find the **area** of these shapes to the nearest **square centimetre.**

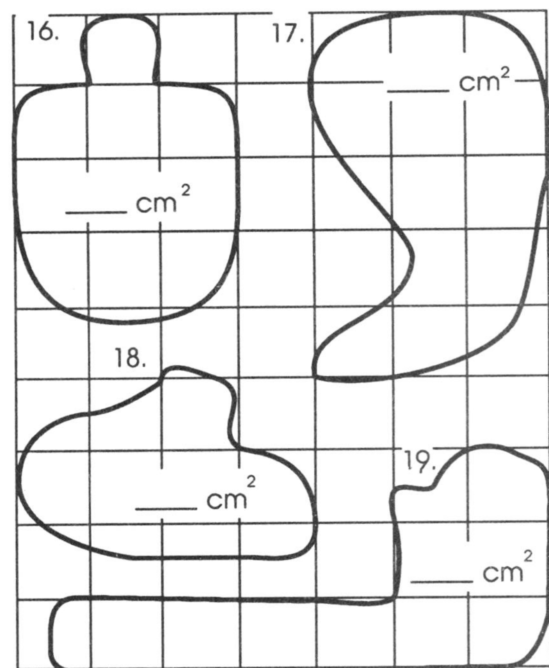

20. What is the area of a playing card? ______

21. Find the surface area of an orange. *(Lay all the skin on 1cm² grid paper.)* ______

22. Measure the surface area of a large book such as an encyclopedia. *(Measure all sides.)* ______

23. Find the area of a houseplant leaf. ______

24. Find the area of any large leaf. ______

Add the correct unit - **square centimetres (cm²)** or **square metres (m²)** to these areas.

25. The playground is 2 000 ______

26. The parking space is 15 ______

27. A book cover is 436 ______

28. A school blackboard is 4 ______

1. 296
 + 143
 ______

2. 354
 + 426
 ______

3. 252
 + 187
 ______

4. 514
 + 378
 ______

5. 634
 + 259
 ______

6. 873
 + 58
 ______

7. 505
 + 456
 ______

8. 89
 + 706
 ______

9. 386
 + 537
 ______

Use a calculator for these, if you need it.

10. 261 + 38 + 154 = ________

11. 408 + 333 + 85 = ________

12. 141 + 411 + 270 + 16 = ________

13. 397 + 74 + 248 + 112 = ________

14. 190 + 324 + 109 - 26 = ________

15. Complete the **addition** web.

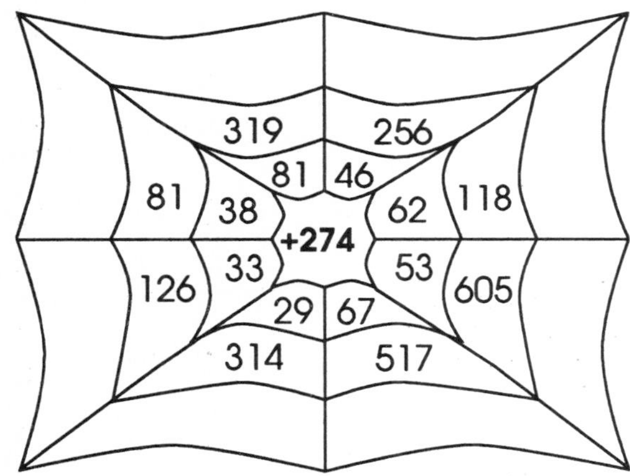

Fill in the gaps in the chains.

16. [91] + [254] + [378] + [27] = [ ]

17. [160] + [278] = [ ] + [102] = [ ]

18. [679] - [143] = [ ] + [27] = [ ]

19. Measure the **surface area** of a car number plate. ________

20. What is the **surface area** of a post card? ________

21. What is the **surface area** of a chair seat? ________

22. 19 + 36 + 14 = ________

23. 39 + 28 + 11 = ________

24. 51 + 33 + 9 = ________

25. 18 + 42 + 27 = ________

26. 25 + 50 + 8 = ________

27. 41 + 15 + 26 = ________

28. 10 + 71 + 11 = ________

29. If it is 60 km by road from Corke to Yarm, and 105 km from Yarm to Groome, how far is it from Corke to Groome? ________

30. It is 97 km from Melton to Seymour and 214 km from Seymour to Albury. How far is it from Melton to Albury? ________

31. What is the area of this irregular shape?

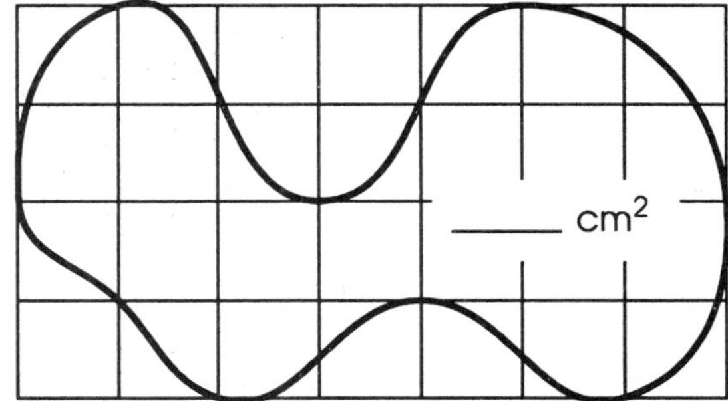

32. 405
 + 163
 ______

33. 519
 + 339
 ______

34. 234
 + 678
 ______

1. 54 - 37 = ______
2. 29 - 16 = ______
3. 38 - 21 = ______
4. 77 - 45 = ______
5. 86 - 39 = ______
6. 66 - 48 = ______
7. 95 - 56 = ______
8. 74 - 47 = ______
9. 58 - 19 = ______
10. 87 - 48 = ______

11. Forty-eight sausage rolls were put out at a party and 25 were eaten. How many left ? ______

12. Ninety-six days were divided into sunny days or dull days. There were 67 sunny days. How many days were dull ? ______

13. Gino had 57 pigeons entered in a race. By 6 o'clock 24 had come home. How many still to come? ______

14. Make up a number story for this **sum.**

____

____

____

____

$$\begin{array}{r} 48 \\ -\,18 \\ \hline \\ \hline \end{array}$$

15. Make up a story for this sum.

76 - 56 = ______ + 12 = ______

____

____

____

____

16. A man has **£ 97** in the bank. He takes out **£ 56** and the bank charges a fee of **£ 3.** How much does he have left in the bank? ______

Draw these shapes below the labels.

17. *Rhombus*

18. *Heptagon*

19. *Octagon*

20. *Nonagon*

21. *Hexagon*

22. *Decagon*

23. Draw an **octagon**, then join each point to all the other points. How many **diagonals** have you drawn? ______

24. On a separate piece of paper draw a **nonagon**, then join each point to all the other points. How many **diagonals** have you drawn? ______

Estimate the **capacity** of containers like these, then measure the **capacity** accurately in **litres** and **millilitres.**

1.  Est. _____ Capacity _______

2. Est. _____ Capacity _______

3  Est. _____ Capacity _______

4. Est. _____ Capacity _______

5.  Est. _____ Capacity _______

6. Est. _____ Capacity _______

Write these measurements in decimal form.

7. 125 millilitres ________________
8. 684 millilitres ________________
9. 1 340 millitres ________________
10. 2 763 millilitres ________________
11. 4 807 millilitres ________________
12. 18 millilitres ________________

Add these **capacities**.

13. 17l + 6l = ________
14. 9l+ 29l = ________
15. 6l + 12l 114ml = ________
16. 9l 592ml + 4l 206ml = ________
17. 14l 671ml + 5l 736ml= ________

18.	19.	20.
7l 250ml	9l 87ml	2l 157ml
9l 376ml	3l 769ml	12l 296ml
+ 4l 50 ml	+ 2l 417ml	+ 9l 815ml

21. Fill in the missing numbers on the **subtraction** wheel.

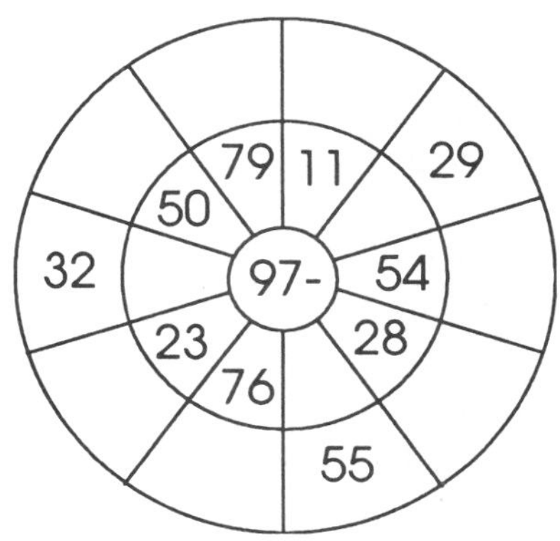

Add these **capacities.**

22. 4l + 2l 375ml +1l + 625ml = __________
23. 2l 240 ml + 4l 460 ml + 750 ml =__________
24. 710 ml + 1l 675 ml + 663 ml =__________
25. 5l 479 ml + 856 ml + 4l 175 ml = __________

26. Draw and record the number of **diagonals** on the **hexagon**.

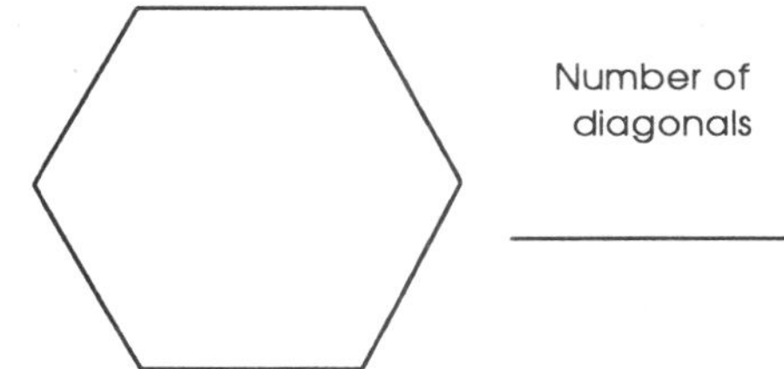

Number of diagonals ________

27. Draw an **octagonal prism**.

Write these as **millilitres**.

28. 1.64 l ________________
29. 2.786 l ________________
30. 0.25 l ________________

A cyclist in training rides these **distances** during a week.

Sunday 29km
Monday 46km
Tuesday 53km
Wednesday 78km
Thursday 84km
Friday 35km
Saturday 31km

1. How many more kilometres did the cyclist ride on Monday than on Sunday? ______

2. What is the difference between the Thursday and Tuesday rides? ______

3. How many more kilometres would have to be ridden on Friday to equal Thursday's distance? ______

4. If the cyclist doubled Saturday's distance, how many kilometres still short of Wednesday's ride? ______

5. How many kilometres ridden altogether during the week? ______

6. Which two days' rides when added together equal Thursday's distance?

________________ ________________

7. Complete the penny-farthing **take aways.**

8. Colour the lines needed to show a **trapezium** on the drawing.

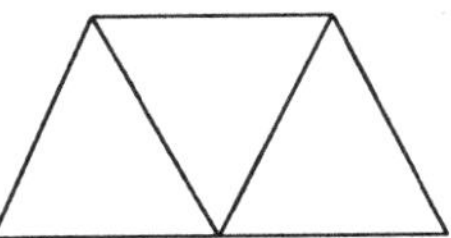

9. Colour the lines needed to show a **rhombus** on this drawing.

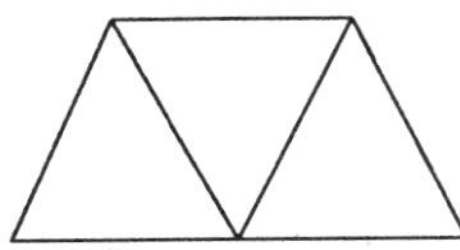

10. Add lines to this drawing to make a **hexagon.**

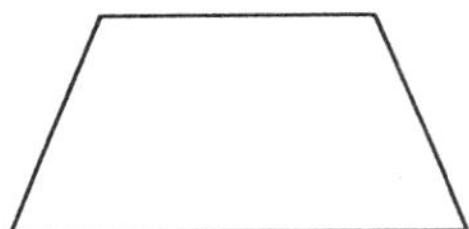

11. Draw a **decagon.**

12. Work out the number of **lines of symmetry** in each **2-D** shape.

(a) 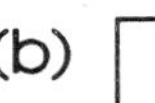 ______

(b)  ______

(c) 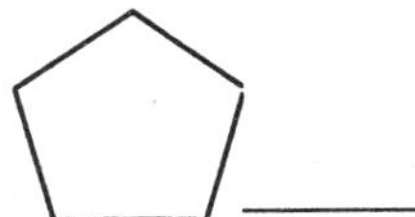 ______

(d)   ______

1. If it is **11°C** at 9.00 a.m. and **27°C** at 1.00 p.m., how far has the **temperature** risen? ________

2. If it is **38°C** at 3.00 p.m. and **9°C** at 11.00 p.m., how far has the **temperature** fallen? ________

Here are the highest **temperatures** recorded each day for a week.

Sun	Mon	Tues	Wed	Thur	Fri	Sat
17°C	22°C	23°C	29°C	33°C	25°C	18°C

3. Show these **temperatures** on the **line graph.**

15°C ————————————→

Here are the **temperature** ranges for some cities during a day in August.

Amsterdam	10°C - 18 °C
Barcelona	13°C - 25°C
Cairo	18°C - 28°C
Calgary	0°C - 18°C
Mecca	26°C - 42°C
Rome	18°C - 25°C
Wellington	7°C - 12°C

4. Name a city where it would be very cold. ____________

5. Name a city where it would be very hot. ____________

6. Name two cities where it would have been pleasant that day.

____________ ____________

7. Mark the **minimum temperatures** for each city on the line graph.

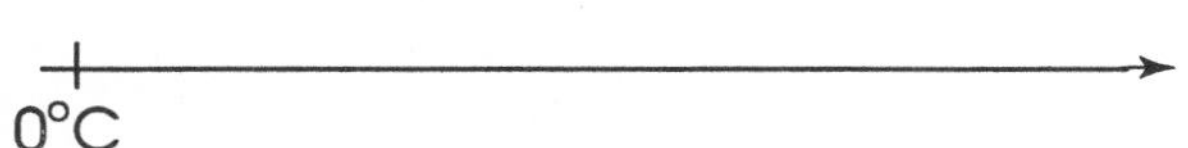

8. Draw all **lines of symmetry** across this **octagon.**

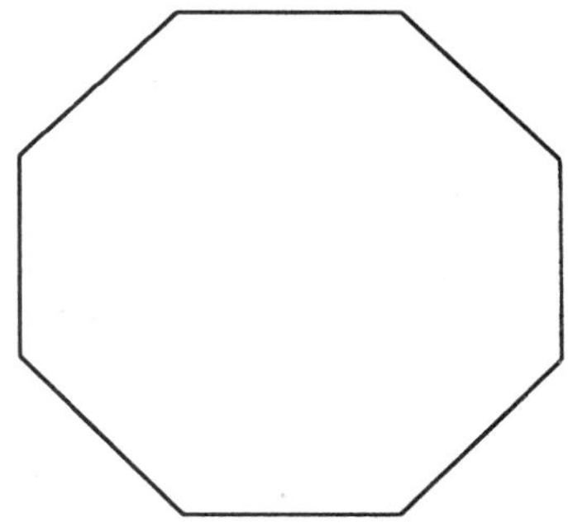

9. 33 - 24 = ______

10. 46 - 29 = ______

11. 98 - 57 = ______

12. 77 - 55 = ______

13. 48 - 19 = ______

14. 54 - 36 = ______

15. 89 - 60 = ______

16. 62 - 16 = ______

17. 38 - 19 = ______

18. 87 - 49 = ______

19. Arrange these **temperatures** in order, highest to lowest.

17°C 8°C 39°C 4°C 27°C 20°C

____

20. What is the difference between the highest and lowest **temperature** above? ________

21. Find out what the **temperature** is now and write it here. ________

22. **Celsius** is known as a **centigrade scale.** Find out what this means.

____

____

____

23. Find out about the **Fahrenheit** temperature scale.
Water freezes at ______ °F.

1. 16
 x 5

2. 27
 x 4

3. 19
 x 5

4. 31
 x 3

5. 48
 x 6

6. 53
 x 7

7. 67
 x 9

8. 53
 x 8

9. 73
 x 9

10. 84
 x 6

11. 100
 x 3

12. 200
 x 6

13. There are 5 rows of 60 chairs in an assembly hall. How many chairs altogether? ________

14. Seventy children were each given 6 packets of biscuits to sell. How many packets? ________

15. If there were 36 biscuits in each packet, how many biscuits for each child? ________

16. If there were 6 red roses in 53 bunches, how many red roses? ________

17. Ben ran 6 km every day during July. How many kilometres did he run? ________

18. 100
 x 7

19. 200
 x 4

20. 200
 x 5

21. Think of this grid as a plan of a table or desk. Draw 6 objects on it, in various positions.

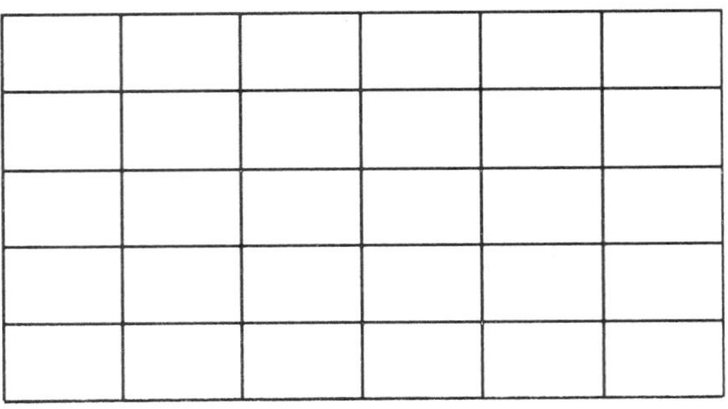

22. This clever bee is going to fly through the rain to the sunflower without getting wet. Draw the path he will take.

23. Draw number and letter references on this grid. Go up A to F, and across 1 to 7, left to right.

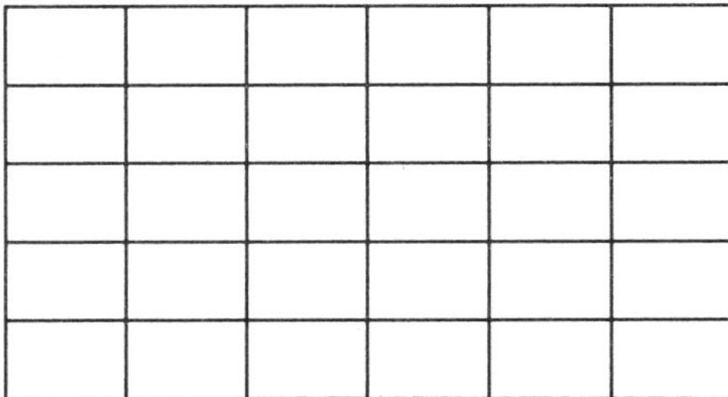

24. Put an X where B and 3 meet.

25. Draw a circle at D5.

26. Draw a small square at E2.

27. Put an X at C4.

28. Draw a small triangle at E6.

1. 42 ÷ 6 = ______
2. 60 ÷ 5 = ______
3. 81 ÷ 9 = ______
4. 56 ÷ 8 = ______
5. 63 ÷ 7 = ______
6. 84 ÷ 4 = ______
7. 36 ÷ 9 = ______
8. 64 ÷ 8 = ______
9. 66 ÷ 6 = ______
10. 55 ÷ 5 = ______

Write the sum for each of these simple problems.

11. Divide 49 trainers into pairs.

_____ ÷ _____ = _____ r _____

12. Fifty-eight marbles shared equally among 7 players. How many each?

_____ ÷ _____ = _____ r _____

13. How many oranges are needed to make 38 quarters?

_____ ÷ _____ = _____ r _____ ☐ oranges

14. Share 90 cherries among 8 children. How many each?

_____ ÷ _____ = _____ r _____

15. Complete the maths garden wall.

Fill in the missing numbers.

16. ____ ÷ 6 = 7
17. 64 ÷ ____ = 16
18. 81 ÷ ____ = 3
19. ____ ÷ 25 = 5

20. 96 shared among 12 = _______

21. $\begin{array}{r} 56 \\ \times\ 4 \\ \hline \end{array}$

22. $\begin{array}{r} 37 \\ \times\ 3 \\ \hline \end{array}$

23. $\begin{array}{r} 42 \\ \times\ 5 \\ \hline \end{array}$

24. $\begin{array}{r} 74 \\ \times\ 6 \\ \hline \end{array}$

25. $\begin{array}{r} 29 \\ \times\ 9 \\ \hline \end{array}$

26. $\begin{array}{r} 35 \\ \times\ 8 \\ \hline \end{array}$

27. Show the path through the maze of squares.

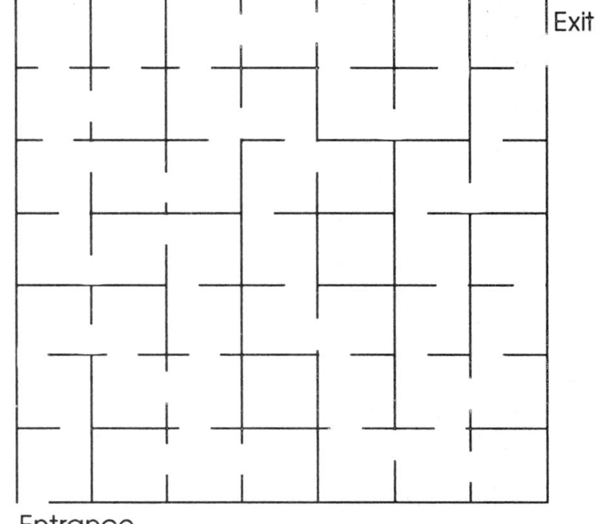

28. 21 ÷ 7 = ______
29. 72 ÷ 8 = ______
30. 60 ÷ 5 = ______
31. 48 ÷ 6 = ______
32. 72 ÷ 9 = ______
33. 42 ÷ 7 = ______
34. 48 ÷ 8 = ______
35. 54 ÷ 9 = ______

Write the grid reference for each shape.

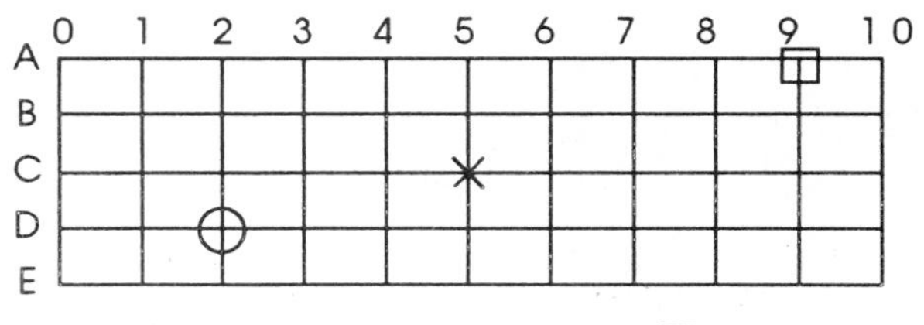

36. ✕ 37. ○ 38. ☐

1. 8) 24   2. 3) 36   3. 9) 27

4. 10) 70   5. 7) 49   6. 6) 48

7. 4) 36   8. 5) 55   9. 9) 81

10. Seventy cakes are to be packed ten to a box. How many boxes are needed? ________

11. Forty-five children are to go to a concert by car. Each car holds 5 children. How many cars are needed? ________

12. Fifty-six litres of petrol are to be divided among 8 boats. How many litres for each boat? ________

13. Forty-two buttons are to be sewn on 6 shirts. How many buttons on each shirt? ________

14. Thirty-nine bread rolls were packed in baker's dozens. How many packs? *Careful!* ________

15. Complete the **division** wheel. Don't forget to fill in any remainders.

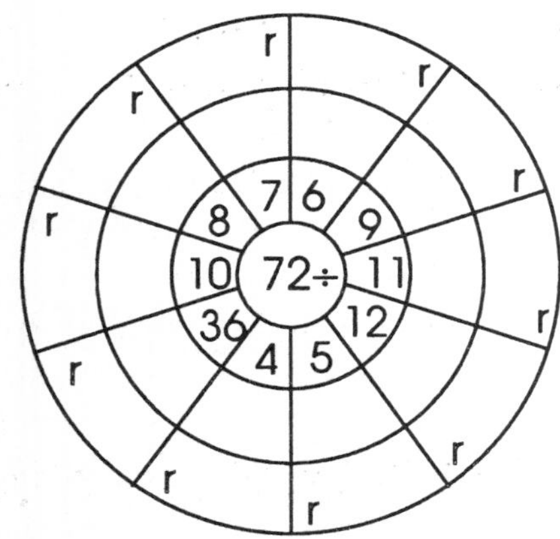

This is a layout of a supermarket. The aisles are marked with numbers and the shelves with letters.

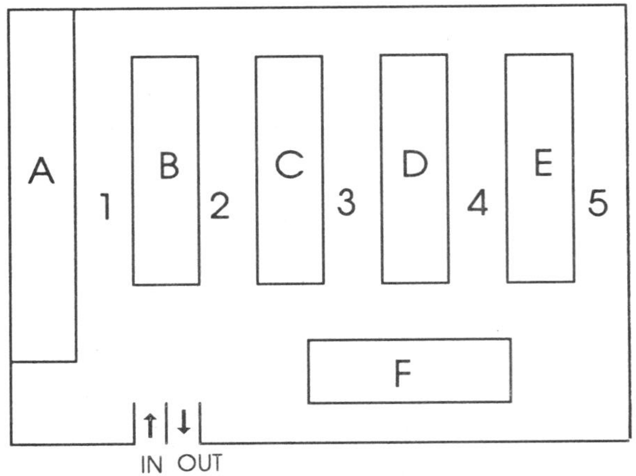

16. What shelf do you see right in front of you as you enter? ________

17. What is the number of the aisle on the far right?________

18. Biscuits are on the furthest half of shelf A. Shade it and write *BISCUITS.*

19. Label shelf C on aisle 3 *VEGETABLES.*

20. Show *PET FOOD* on Shelf E at the far end facing the wall.

21. Shelf F is frozen food. Label it.

22. Show the following route around the supermarket by drawing a line.

> *Go down aisle 1 to the end, go right to aisle 4, go along aisle 4. Move around to aisle 5, to the far end, and finally walk to aisle 2 and along to the check-out.*

23. Put an **X** at the near end of shelf C to show the special offers.

1. What is the **temperature** of a glass of tap water? _______

2. What is the temperature of a glass of hot water from a tap? _______

3. Estimate, then check with a thermometer the outside temperature. _______

4. Record the **average** daytime temperature where you live. _______

5. A meat dish is to be cooked at 200°C. The thermometer on the oven reads 170°C. By how many degrees does the temperature need to rise to cook the dish? _______

Read each of these **thermometers.**

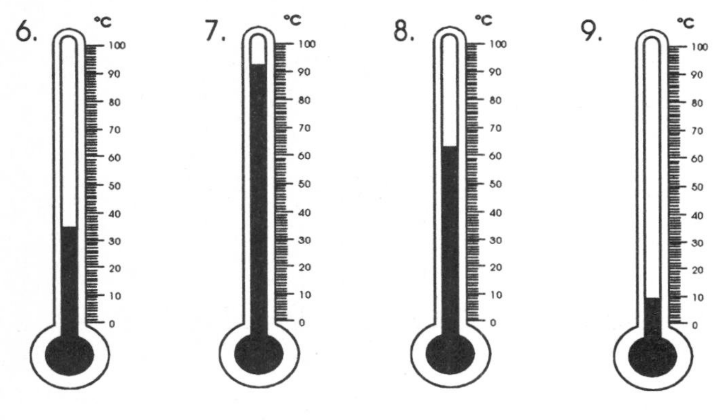

6. _______ 7. _______ 8. _______ 9. _______

Mark the **thermometers** to show the **temperatures.**

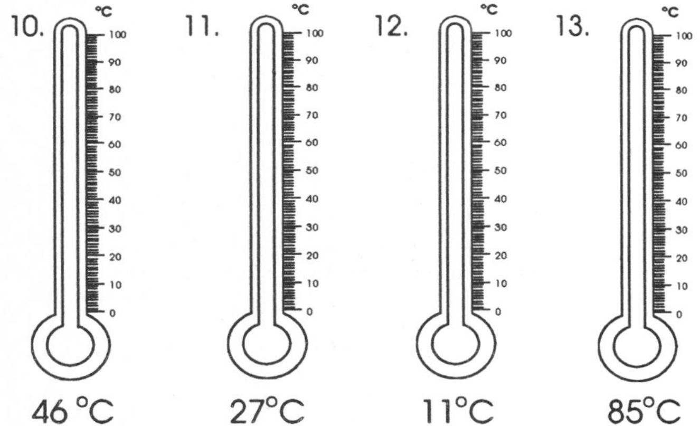

10. 46 °C 11. 27°C 12. 11°C 13. 85°C

14. What is the difference between body **temperature** and boiling water in **degrees Celsius?** _______

15. This is a jumbo game of noughts and crosses. Fill in the **grid** to see who wins.

0	A1	B2	B4	C1	C3	C4	D2	D3
X	A2	A3	A4	B1	B3	C2	D1	D4

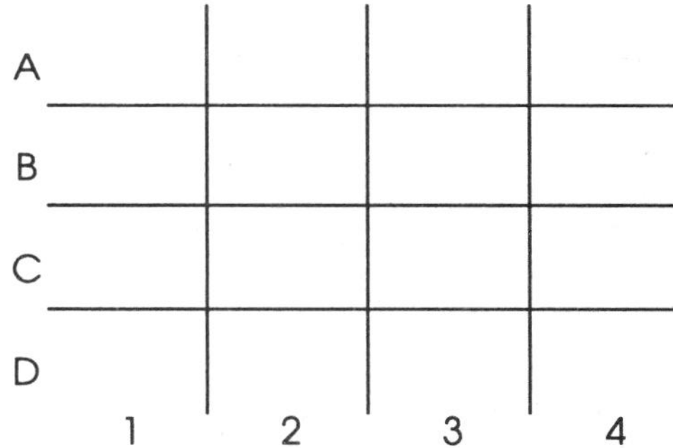

Who won, 0 or X? _______

16. $10\overline{)60}$

17. $9\overline{)36}$

18. $8\overline{)72}$

19. $7\overline{)56}$

20. $9\overline{)63}$

21. $3\overline{)81}$

22. Eighty kilograms of fertilizer are put in 9kg bags. How many full bags and how many kilograms left over?

_______ full bags _______kg left over

23. A service station fills 6l oil cans from a 45 litre drum. How many full cans and how much left in the drum?

_______full bottles _______ l left

24. Pack 67 oranges into bags of 8. How many full bags and how many oranges left over?

_______full bags_______left over

25. Seventy-seven children were divided into groups of 7. How many groups? _______

Unit 11

Colour the ladders to show the **fraction**, then write the **decimal** .

1. 7 tenths 0.______
2. 4 tenths 0.______
3. 9 tenths 0.______
4. 3 tenths 0.______
5. 5 tenths 0.______
6. 2 tenths 0.______

7. Change these **hundredths** to **percentages**.

(a) 70 hundredths __________%

(b) 85 hundredths __________%

(c) 56 hundredths __________%

(d) 49 hundredths __________%

(e) 3 hundredths __________%

8. Change these decimal **fractions** into **units**, **tenths** and **hundredths.**

Fraction	Units	Tenths	Hundredths
0.40			
0.37			
1.86			
0.05			
3.33			

9. How many hundredths are shaded on the grid ? ________

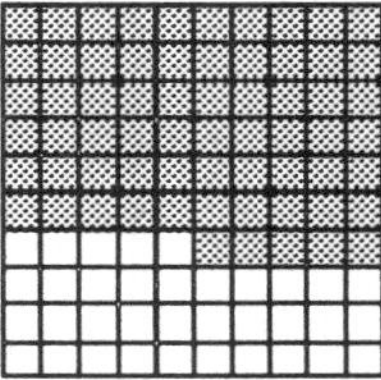

10. How many more should be shaded to make 7 tenths ? ________

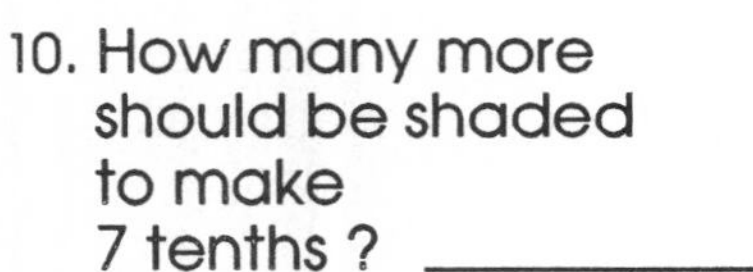

11. Make a picture graph to show the number of animals seen at the children's zoo.

8 sheep	4 cows	6 kangaroos
2 peacocks	5 goats	7 rabbits

Here is a picture graph of objects seen on a train trip.

12. How many lorries were seen? ______

13. How many more trees than barns? ______

14. How many tractors? ______

15. How many barns and cars added together? ______

16. How many cows? ______

17. 6 milk tankers were not added to the picture graph. Put them in.

18. How many objects altogether are now shown on the graph? ______

1. A fortnight = ________ days

2. Eight minutes = ________ seconds

3. Three hours = ________ minutes

4. Two days = ________ hours

5. The month of April has ________ days

6. There are ________ months in 5 years

7. Two decades = ________ years

8. Four centuries = ________ years

9. From 250 B.C. to A.D.1295 ________ years

10. A.D. 1788 was ________ years ago

11. How many days between 20th June and 26th July? ________

12. How long between 9:45 a.m. and 3:20 p.m. the same day? ________

13. How long between 10:37 p.m. and 7:18 a.m. the next day ? ________

These clocks show **24 hour time**. Show the time on the **analog** clocks.

14.

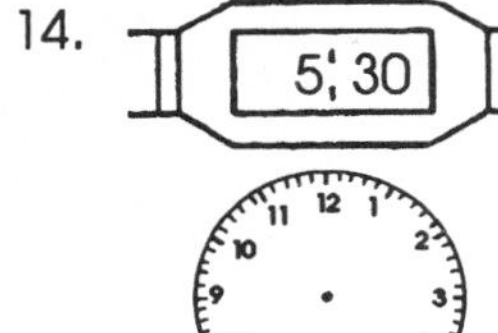

15.

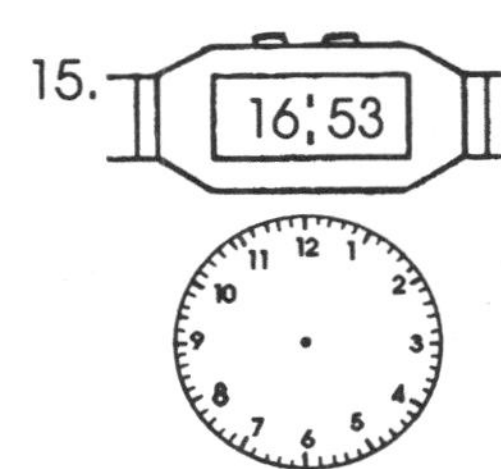

16.

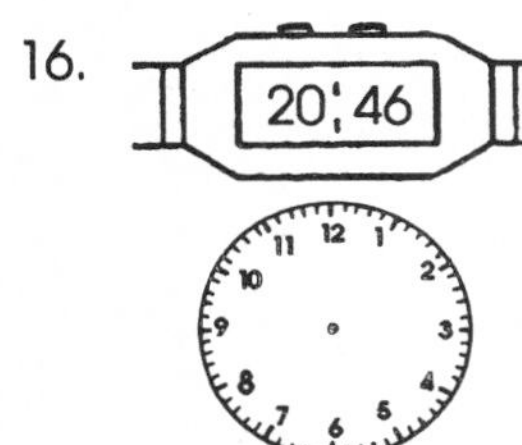

17.

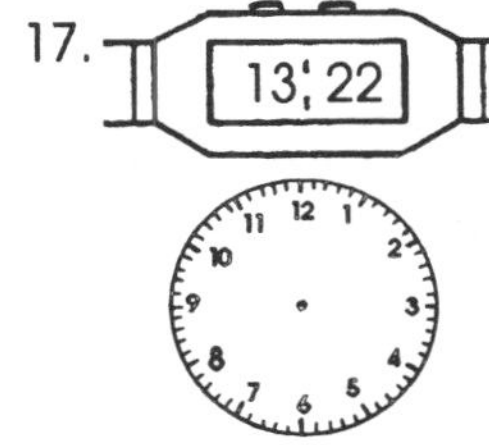

18. How many days in three lunar months ? ________

Change the **hundredths** to **percentages**.

19. 60 hundredths ________ %

20. 18 hundredths ________ %

21. 75 hundredths ________ %

22. 27 hundredths ________ %

23. 43 hundredths ________ %

24. 8 hundredths ________ %

Bronwyn said: "My mother was 30 in 1988, and I was 4."

25. How old is her mother now ? ________

26. How old is Bronwyn now ? ________

27. In what year was her mother born ? ________

28. In what year was Bronwyn born ? ________

29. Captain Cook was born in 1729. He died in 1779. How old was he ? ________

30. Where did he die ? ________

31. How long between the 7:57 a.m. train and the 9:18 a.m. one ? ________

32. How many years between 136 B.C. and A.D. 954 ? ________

33. A woman in Rome died in A.D. 23. She was 71 years old. In what year was she born ? ________

Write these decimal fractions.

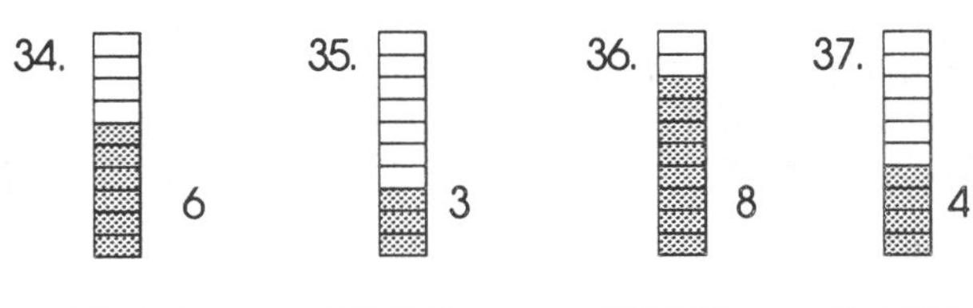

38. Write the next three numbers in this sequence (pattern).

2 4 3 5 4 6 5 7 ____ ____ ____

Write these **hundredths** as **percentages**.

1. $\frac{70}{100}$ _______ %
2. $\frac{41}{100}$ _______ %
3. $\frac{17}{100}$ _______ %
4. $\frac{68}{100}$ _______ %
5. $\frac{95}{100}$ _______ %
6. $\frac{50}{100}$ _______ %

Complete the **fractions** table.

	Hundredths	Over 100	Decimals	%
	45	$\frac{45}{100}$	0.45	45%
7.		$\frac{38}{100}$		
8.			0.8	
9.	17			
10.				56%
11.	73			

12. Write 50% in another way. _______

13. What is another way of writing 25% ? _______

14. Write $\frac{6}{10}$ as a percentage. _______

15. What is the discount price of roller blades at 50% off the normal price off £100 ? _______

16. In a soccer club of 100 members 75% wore the correct uniform. How many were correctly dressed ? _______

17. In a bag of 45 wine gums, 13 were red, 17 green and 8 yellow. What fraction were other colours ? _______

18. Find 5 examples of percentages in a newspaper. Paste them on a sheet of paper, then talk about them with your friends.

19. Record how long it takes you to walk one kilometre. _______

20. Beginning at your school or home, record places which are :

    (a) A quarter of a kilometre away _______

    (b) Half a kilometre away _______

    (c) Three-quarters of a kilometre away _______

    (d) One kilometre away _______

Find distances using the scale.

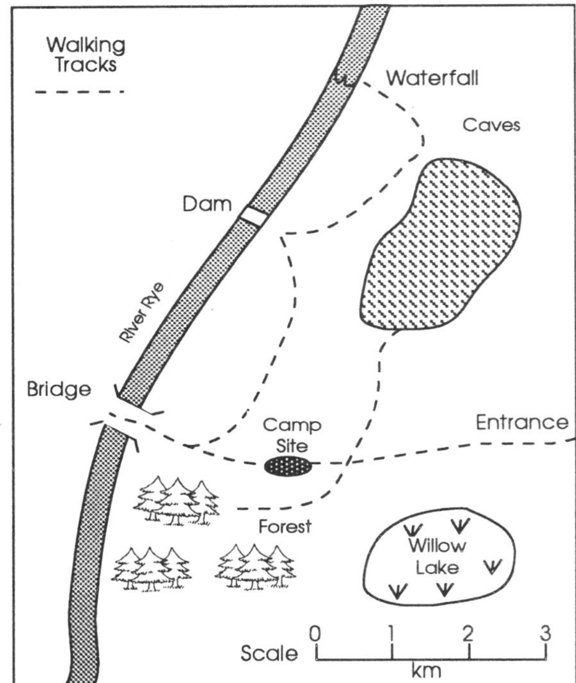

21. From the entrance to the camp site. _______

22. Between the bridge and dam. _______

23. Between the dam and waterfall. _______

24. How far would it be to walk around Willow Lake ? _______

25. What is the length of the river as shown on the map ? _______

26. Could you walk and see everything on this map in one day? _______

1. How many **£5** notes in £100? _______

2. If you gave **£100** for an item worth **£55**, list 3 different sets of notes that might be given as change.

   __________ __________ __________

3. What single note has the same value as these - one £20, four £5 and one £10 note ? _______

4. Write in numbers, seven hundred and forty-five pounds and seventy-five pence. _______

5. Write in words £326.45 ______________

   ____

   ____

This is a supermarket receipt.

Thank you for shopping at ALLWAYS	£
SHORTBREAD BISC	0.62
DETERGENT	1.53
VINEGAR MALT	0.48
COTTON BUDS	0.42
RAISINS 1KG	1.30
LAWN FERTIL.	3.30
SLICED BREAD	0.59
CREAM	0.67
FROZ. CHICK	3.98
YOGURT	1.15
BAL	_______
CASH	_______
CHANGE	_______

6. Find the total balance and fill it in.

7. Fill in the note or notes you would tender as CASH.

8. Fill in the change.

9. If you just bought vinegar, raisins and sliced bread, what would your total be ? _______

10. If you bought a frozen chicken, lawn fertilizer, detergent and yogurt, what would be the total ? _______

Write each of these **percentages** in another way.

11. 17 % _______ 12. 46 % _______

13. 89 % _______ 14. 60 % _______

15. Write $\frac{4}{10}$ in two other ways. __________ __________

16. Write $\frac{7}{10}$ in two other ways. __________ __________

17. Out of 50 cherries, 19 were bad. What **percentage** were edible? _____

18. Out of 100 cakes 45 % were iced. How many were not iced ? _______

19. Out of 25 children, 20 could swim. What **percentage** were non-swimmers ? _______

20. At a shoe shop sale, 81 pairs were black and 19 pairs were brown. Write the brown shoes as a decimal fraction of the total number. _______

21. What four notes make £ 85 ?

    _______ _______ _______ _______

22. Seven notes add up to make £ 75. What are they ? _____ _____

    _____ _____ _____ _____ _____

23. A portable tape recorder is for sale at £ 100 less 122% discount for cash. What change would I receive if I gave £ 100? _______

Add these amounts.

24.	25.	26.
£ 3.60	£ 10.42	£ 6.58
5.05	9.76	5.31
1.27	4.30	.24
_______	_______	_______

Unit 13

Write these numbers in **ascending** order.

1. 7 491 11 076 78 542 8 064 64 020

____

2. 89 741 38 316 8 074 51 746 32 741

____

3. 27 480 27 316 27 614 27 804 27 061

____

4. 73 703 73 007 73 003 73 030 73 300

____

5. 80 416 8 416 84 016 84 610 84 006

____

Name the value of each number in bold.

6. 8**7** 953 ______________
7. **9**1 062 ______________
8. 17 28**4** ______________
9. 54 6**6**0 ______________
10. 27 **3**19 ______________

11. Write these numbers in **descending** order.

72 816 78 618 76 188 76 617 78 861

____

12. Fill in the spaces.

25 000 = ______hundreds =______ tens

13. Write the number after 79 999. ______

14. Write the number before 11 100. ______

15. What number is represented on the electricity meter?

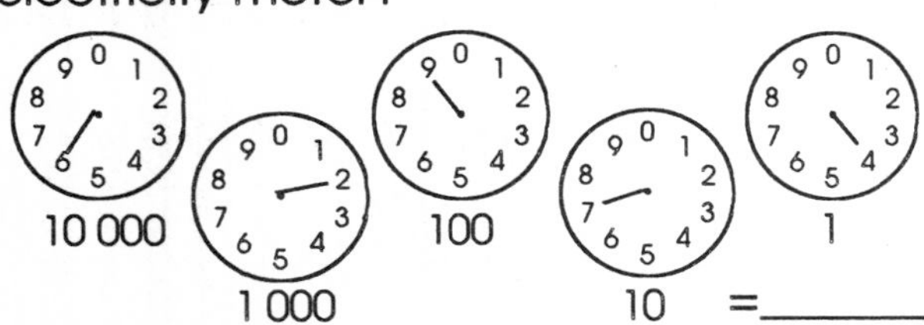

= ________

Here is a survey of drinks children like the most, in tally form.

Kola Fizz	𝍸 IIII	*Hot Chocko*	𝍸 I
Lemonade	IIII	*Orange Pop*	𝍸
Lime Cordial	II	*Banana Shake*	𝍸 I

16. Use this grid to turn the results of the survey into a graph.

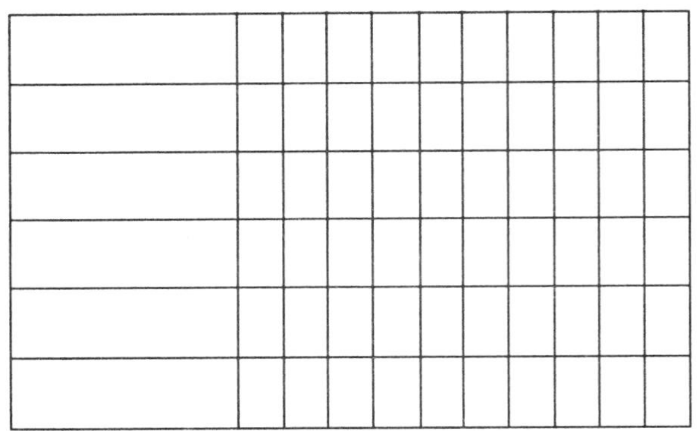

This graph shows the approximate populations of Petsville.

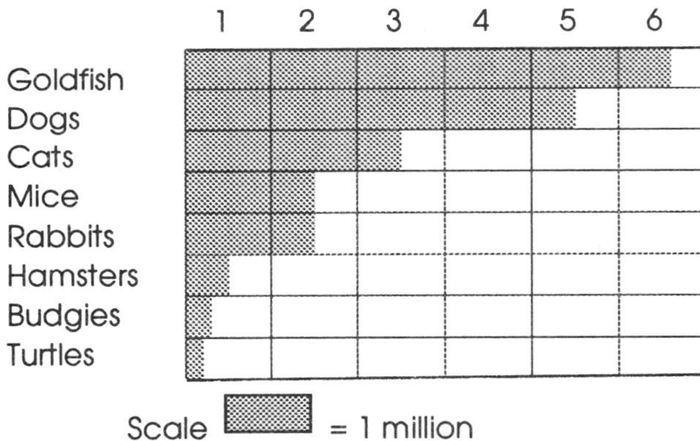

Scale = 1 million

17. Which pets are there most of? ________

18. Which pets are there least of? ________

19. What is the approximate total population of Petsville? ________

20. If you added the goldfish and the dogs together, about what fraction of the total would this be? ________

21. What is the combined population of mice and rabbits? ________

Write these distances in decimal form.

1. 7 kilometres 256 metres ________
2. 15 kilometres 724 metres ________
3. 11 kilometres 19 metres ________
4. 180 kilometres 880 metres ________
5. 960 metres ________

Convert these distances.

6. 6 km = ______m
7. 1560 m = ______km
8. 1431 cm = ______m
9. $\frac{1}{2}$ m = ______ cm
10. $\frac{3}{4}$ km = ______m
11. 150 cm = ______ m

Help fill in the map of Deep Hollow.

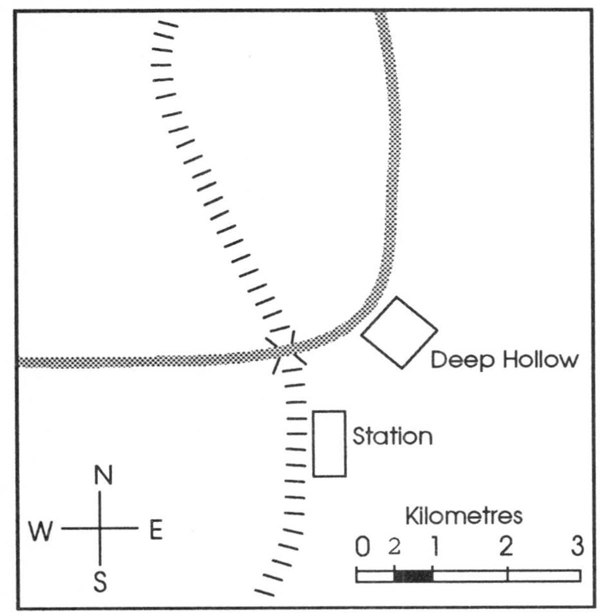

12. Five kilometres north-west of Deep Hollow station is Fernley Station. Show this.
13. 3 kilometres south of the station is the old mining town of Coalville. Show this.
14. There is a road between Coalville and Fernley Station. Show this.
15. How long is this road? ________
16. Four kilometres along the road north of Deep Hollow is Mary's Cafe. Show this.

Write the value of the numbers in bold.

17. 1**9** 426 ____________________
18. **7**3 105 ____________________
19. **4** 028 ____________________
20. 68 **5**13 ____________________
21. 50 0**4**7 ____________________

Convert these distances.

22. 2 850 m = ______ km
23. 768 cm = ______ m
24. $6\frac{1}{2}$ km = ______ m
25. $3\frac{1}{4}$ m = ______cm
26. 900 m = ______ km
27. 10 cm = ______ m

28. Write these numbers in **ascending** order.

58 902 52 805 58 962 52 298

____

29. Write these numbers in **descending** order.

34 716 31 674 31 746 34 167

____

Write these in decimal form.

30. 6km 340m =______
31. 11km 725m =______
32. 3km 440m =______
33. 5km 222m =______

34. Write the numbers 50 before.

(a) 6 143 ________ (b) 825 ________

(c) 1 111 ________ (d) 1 637 ________

35. Write the numbers 50 after.

(a) 3 775 ________ (b) 6 151 ________

(c) 88 888 ________ (d) 7 367________

36. Write the next 3 numbers in this sequence.

1 3 5 4 3 2 4 6 8 7 6 5 ____ ____ ____

1.
```
  413
   25
+ 137
-----
```

2.
```
  213
  506
+  18
-----
```

3.
```
  693
  124
+  72
-----
```

4.
```
  214
  267
+  14
-----
```

5.
```
  384
  207
+ 160
-----
```

6.
```
  273
  324
+ 169
-----
```

7.
```
  458
  261
+ 204
-----
```

8.
```
  346
  295
+ 352
-----
```

9.
```
  472
   17
+ 427
-----
```

10. The school cricket team scored 127, 203 and 174 in three matches. What is the total number of runs scored? ______

11. Add the prices of these goods.

A camera	£178
A telescope	£265
A computer printer	£207

Total price ______

12. Four batches of books came to the library - 98, 174, 235 and 106. How many books altogether? ______

13. For every £50 spent, I receive a £5 discount. If I spend £450, how much discount do I receive? ______

14. What price do I pay? ______

15. What percentage discount is this? ______

Draw the top and side views of each of these **prisms**.

16.

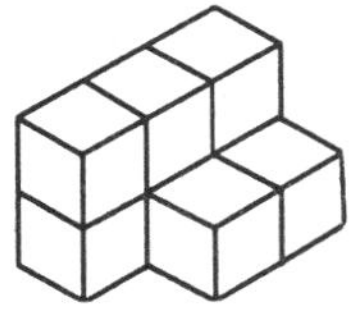

17.

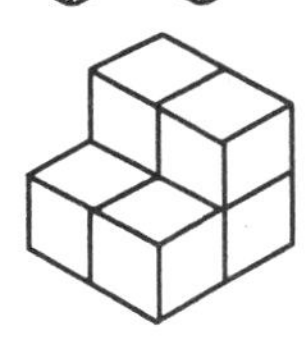

18.

	Top view	Side view
16.		
17.		
18.		

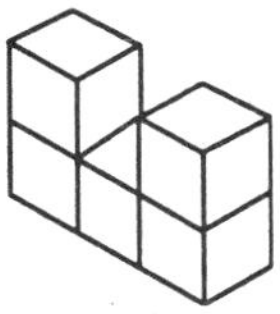

Count the cubes in each of these **prisms**.

19.
______

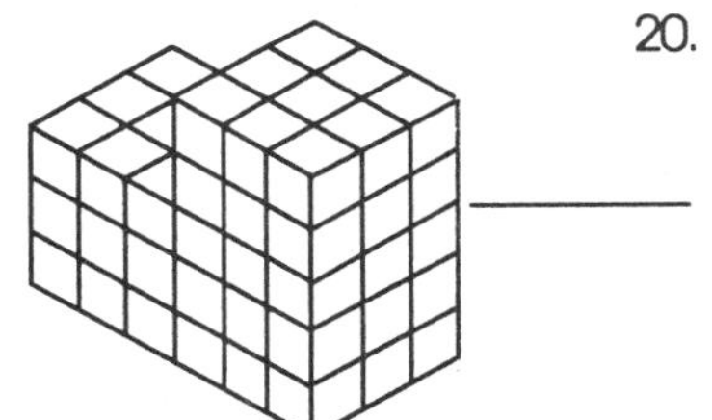

20.
______

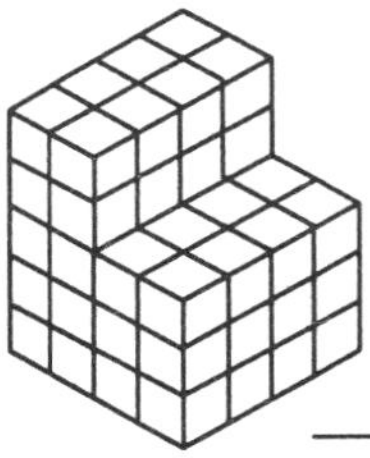

21.
______

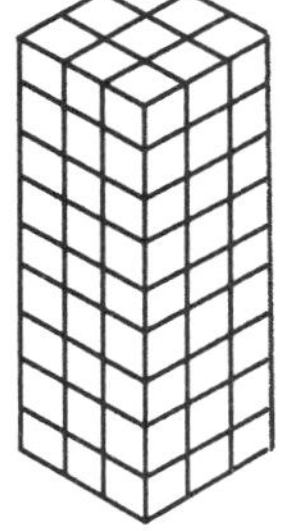

22.
______

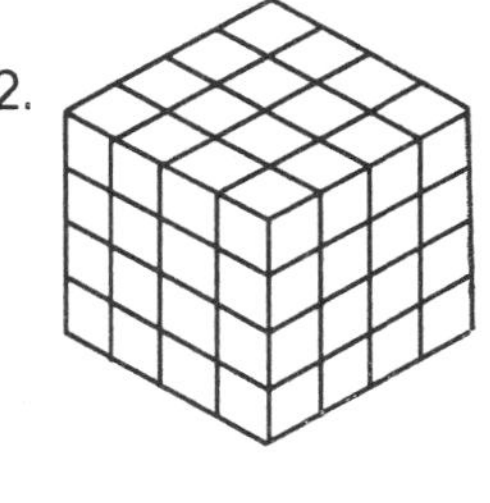

23. This prism is made of 7 cubes. Make and draw two other **prisms** using 7 cubes.

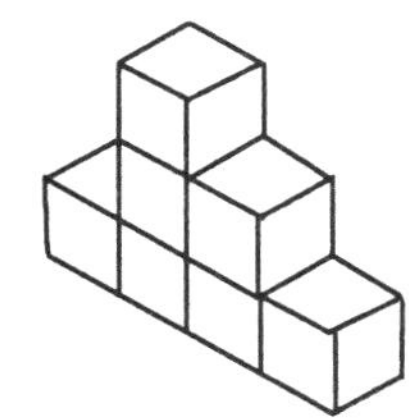

1. 257
 - 136

2. 349
 - 228

3. 416
 - 327

4. 658
 - 329

5. 709
 - 433

6. 872
 - 314

7. 954
 - 667

8. 543
 - 409

9. 866
 - 377

10. Simon's big brother needed £650 for a motorbike. He only had £529. How much did he need to borrow? ______

11. 879 children are enrolled at Deeping school. 451 are girls; how many boys? ______

12. At Deeping hospital, 733 babies were born last year, and the year before 569 babies. How many more last year? ______

13. Deeping cinema can hold 946 people. Last night 777 people went to see a film. How many empty seats were there? ______

14. Of the 777, 238 were children. How many adults? ______

15. Make up a subtraction story that fits the sum.

______
______
______
______

Sum
  651
 - 178

16. 463
  51
 + 174

17. 509
  130
 + 298

18. 249
  413
 + 155

19. Add £212, £183 and £234. What change from £700? ______

20. Add 116g, 306g and 97g. How many grams needed to make 600 grams? ______

21. A truck driver travelled 87km, then 127km and 264km doing deliveries. His truck will travel 700 kilometres on a full tank. How much further can he go? ______

22. Add the numbers in the top line to those down the side.

+	365	164	247
257			
158			

23. Add 425 one-eyed bugs to 156 two-eyed bugs and 230 spotted beetles to total the creepy-crawlies. ______

24. 609
 - 126

25. 528
 - 374

26. 345
 - 249

27. Some road signs give distances in miles. How many kilometres are equal to 1 mile? ______

28. A motorway sign says **London 100 miles.** How far in kilometres? ______

1. Complete the **subtraction** wheel.

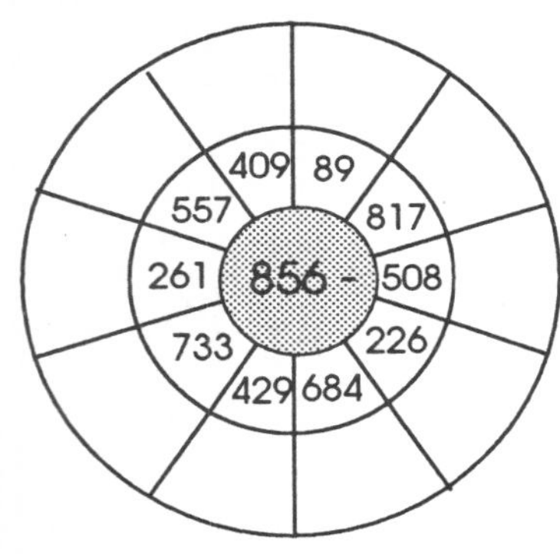

Fill in the missing numbers.

2. 3 1 __
- 2 7 6
4 3

3. 4 __ 1
- __ 6 2
1 1 9

4. 6 4 __
- __ 6 3
1 __ 5

5. __ 9 __
- 5 __ 7
3 8 9

6. 9 __ 4
- __ 1 7
6 7 __

7. A water trough holds 879 litres. If it needs 435 litres to fill it, how much does it already hold? ______

8. It takes 32 hours to travel to Deeping and 24 hours to travel to Fernley. How much longer in minutes to travel to Deeping? ______

A chemist measures out 696 grams of yellow powder and 348 grams of blue powder.

9. What is the difference in grams? ______

10. What fraction is the blue powder of the yellow powder? ______

11. What is the weight of powder when the two are mixed? ______

12. What fraction is the blue powder of the whole mixture? ______

13. How many more grams than a kilogram is the whole mixture? ______

Angles can be labelled in five ways - **straight, acute, obtuse, reflex** and **right angles**. Label these angles.

14. 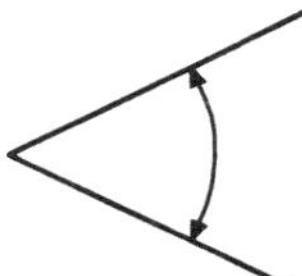 ______

15. ______

16. 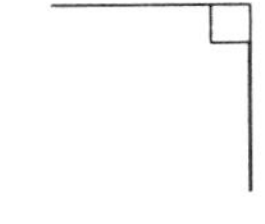 ______

17. 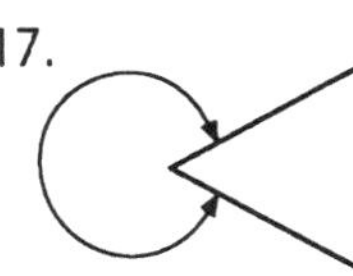 ______

18. ______

19. 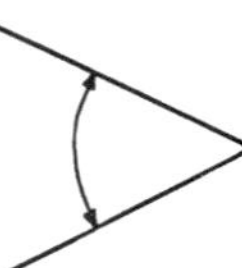 ______

20. 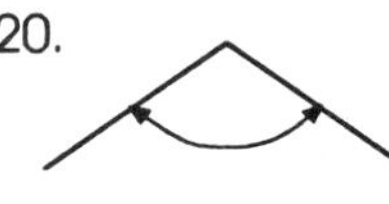 ______

21. 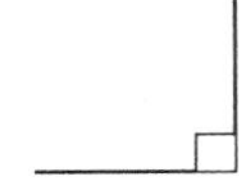 ______

22. 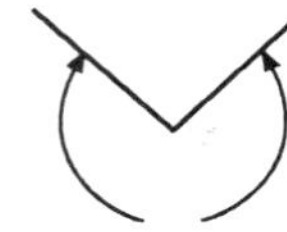 ______

23. What are the angles in an **octagon**? ______

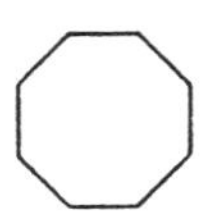

24. What are the two types of angles in a **rhombus**?

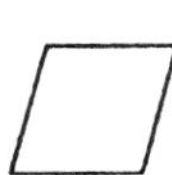

(a) ______

(b) ______

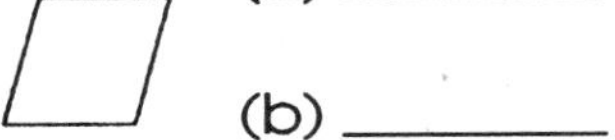

25. What angles make up this **triangle**?

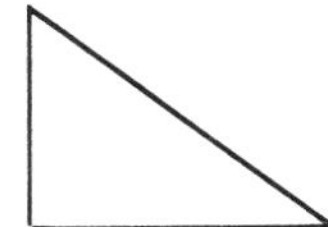

(a) ______

(b) ______ (c) ______

26. What angles make up this **triangle**?

(a) ______

(b) ______ (c) ______

27. List the types of angles here and say how many there are of each.

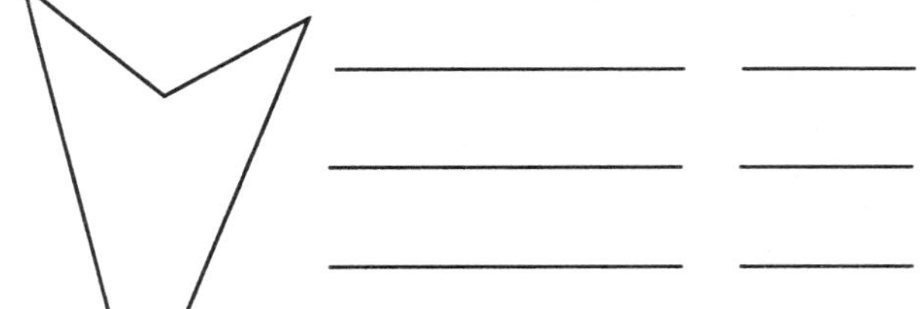

1. How many square centimetres in a square metre? ________

2. How many square metres in a hectare? ________

3. How many hectares in a square kilometre? ________

4. List three areas you know that are about one hectare.

   (a) ________________________________

   (b) ________________________________

   (c) ________________________________

5. List three things that measure about one square kilometre.

   (a) ________________________________

   (b) ________________________________

   (c) ________________________________

6. A small farm is for sale and is advertised as being 50 ha. What is this in square kilometres? ________

7. In mapping a big national park, what unit of area would you use?

   ____

8. What does **boundary** mean?

   ____

   ____

9. Find out about 'old' measures of land area. How many square yards in an acre? ________

10. About how many acres are equal to a hectare? ________

11. A road runs from Deeping to the sea and is 349 km long. It is 166 km further from Deeping to Fernley. How far from Fernley to the sea? ________

12. Of a 481ha development site 190ha is to be set aside as common land. How much is left for housing? ________

13. A length of timber is 4m 56cm. 97cm is cut off. How much left? ________

14. 826 − 519 = ___ ___ ___

15. ___07 − 386 = ___121

16. 688 − 4___1 = 197

17. ___34 − 511 = 22___

18. 9___5 − ___44 = 311

19. 4___9 − ___05 = 18___

20. Label these angles R (right), A (acute), O (obtuse), or Rx (reflex).

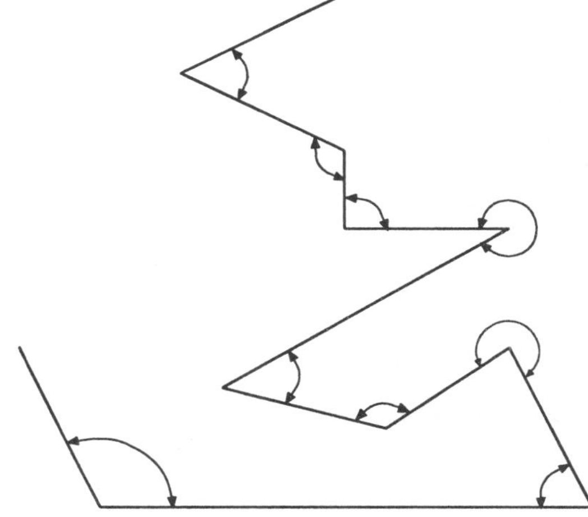

21. Draw a shape with 5 obtuse angles.

22. Draw a shape with 3 acute angles.

1. 24 x 4 = ______

2. 145 x 3 = ______

3. 205 x 6 = ______

4. 117 x 8 = ______

5. 237 x 3 = ______

6. 115 x 4 = ______

7. 225 x 5 = ______

8. 156 x 7 = ______

A school is choosing a new uniform for girls. The **choice** has to be from:

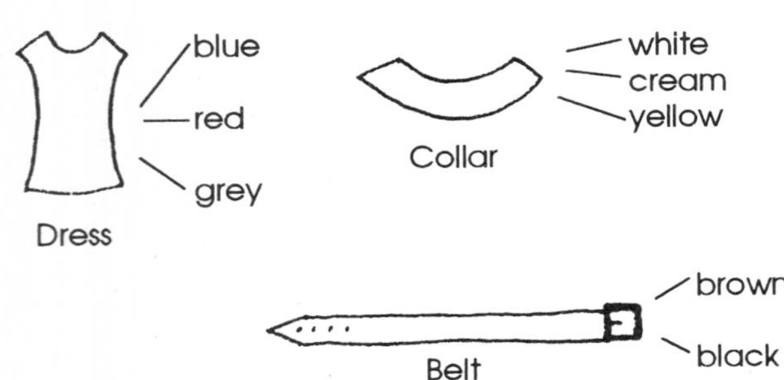

9. How many different **combinations** of dress, collar and belt can you find? ______

The same school is choosing a uniform for boys. The **choices** are to be made from:

10. How many **combinations?** ______

11. Out of all the **combinations** which would you **choose?**

______

______

______

______

12. 232 x 5 = ______ + 16 = ______

13. Find six **right angles** in your home or classroom.

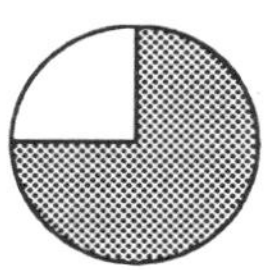

(a) ______

(b) ______

(c) ______

(d) ______

(e) ______

(f) ______

14. How many **right angles** would complete a circle? ______

15. How many **right angles** does a square have? ______

16. Order these angles 1 to 5, smallest to largest.

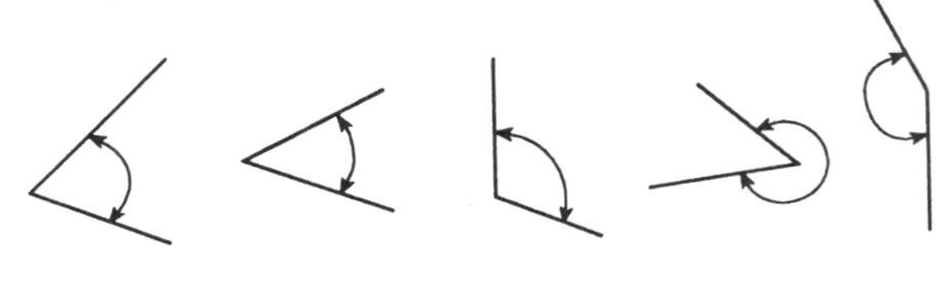

______ ______ ______ ______ ______

17. How many **obtuse** angles in a hexagon? ______

18. How many **acute** angles in a rectangle? ______

19. How many **right angles** in an equilateral (all sides the same) triangle? ______

20. Mark the angles in this shape **R** (right angle), **A** (acute) or **O** (obtuse).

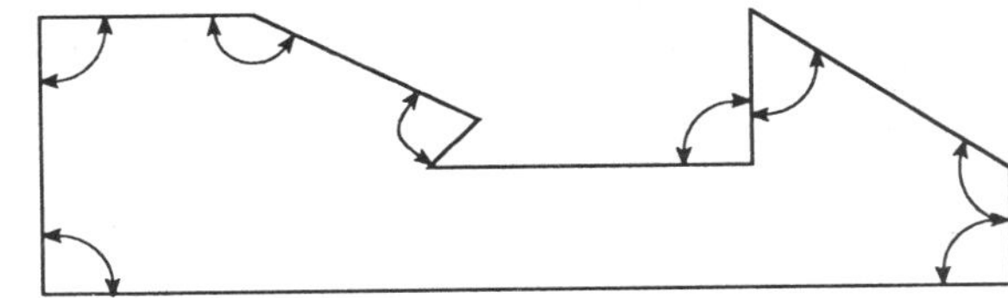

1. Draw a **cubic centimetre.**

2. Write the abbreviation for **cubic centimetre.** ________

Build these prisms using 1cm cubes, and give the **volume** in **cm³**.

	Length	Width	Height	cm³
3.	3cm	2cm	1cm	
4.	3cm	3cm	2cm	
5.	2cm	3cm	2cm	
6.	4cm	2cm	2cm	
7.	4cm	3cm	2cm	
8.	5cm	4cm	2cm	
9.	4cm	5cm	3cm	
10.	4cm	4cm	3cm	

Look at each prism, then count the cubes to work out the volume in **cm³**.

11. 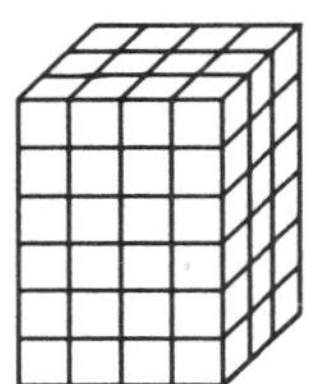
____

12. 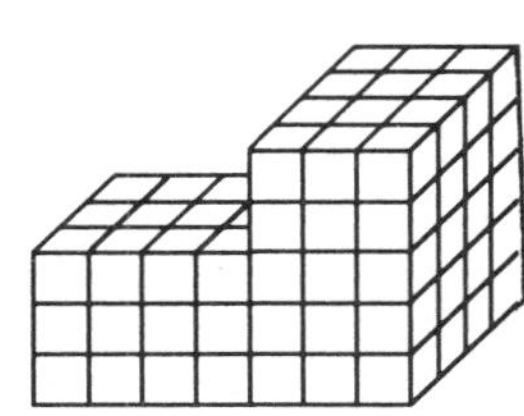
____

13. 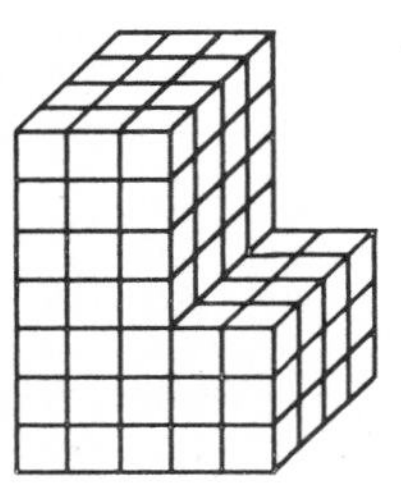
____

14. 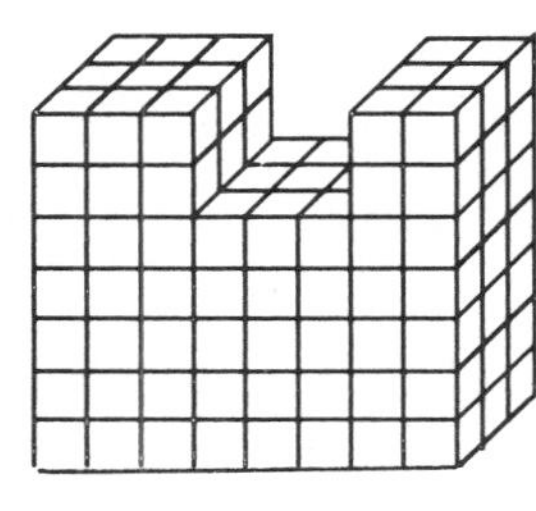
____

15. Children are allowed 2 pieces of fruit, one from the first group and one from the second group. How many combinations are there?

16. List 2 combinations you might choose.

(a) ________________

(b) ________________

17. 36 x3 ________

18. 120 x 4 ________

19. 154 x 5 ________

20. 130 x6 ________

21. 308 x 2 ________

22. 90 x 8 ________

23. 75 x 9 ________

24. 218 x4 ________

25. 171 x 5 ________

26. What is the **volume** of a **prism** whose sides are: length 5cm, width 3cm and height 2cm? ________

27. A **prism** has these sides: length 4cm, width 6cm and height 3cm. What is its **volume?** ________

28. What is the **volume** of this object in **cm³?**

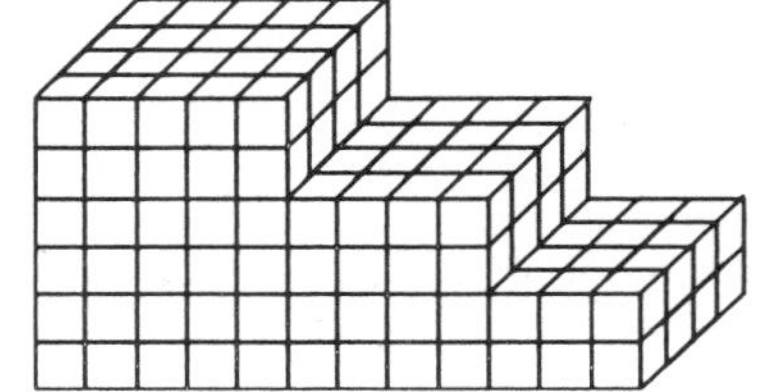

____

1. 49 ÷ 7 = _____

2. 72 ÷ 8 = _____

3. 96 ÷ 12 = _____

4. 121 ÷ 11 = _____

5. 45 ÷ 5 = _____

6. 108 ÷ 9 = _____

7. 3) 93

8. 7) 56

9. 4) 88

10. 16) 64

11. 9) 63

12. 3) 51

Watch for the remainders.

13. 9) 47 r

14. 8) 75 r

15. 7) 68 r

16. Ninety marbles are to be shared among ten children. How many each? _____

17. Eighty-three scones placed equally on 8 plates. How many on each plate, and how many left over?

_____ plate _____ left over

18. Liam has a 96 page book which he wants to read over 7 nights. How many pages each night? Any pages left still to read?

_____ pages per night _____ still to read

19. One-hundred and one marbles shared among four children. How many each? Any left over?

_____ marbles _____ left over

20. Complete the **division** table.

÷	96	64	112	32	80	48	16
8							
16							

21. Show these points of interest on the map of Lord Howe Island using the co-ordinates.

(a) *Airstrip* E7.5
(b) *Mt Eliza* B10
(c) *Mt Lidgbird* F4
(d) *Mt Gower* E2
(e) *Ned's Beach* D10
(f) *Rabbit Island* C8
(g) *Blinky Beach* F7
(h) *Red Point* G3.5
(i) *Big Slopes* E1
(j) *The Saddles* F3

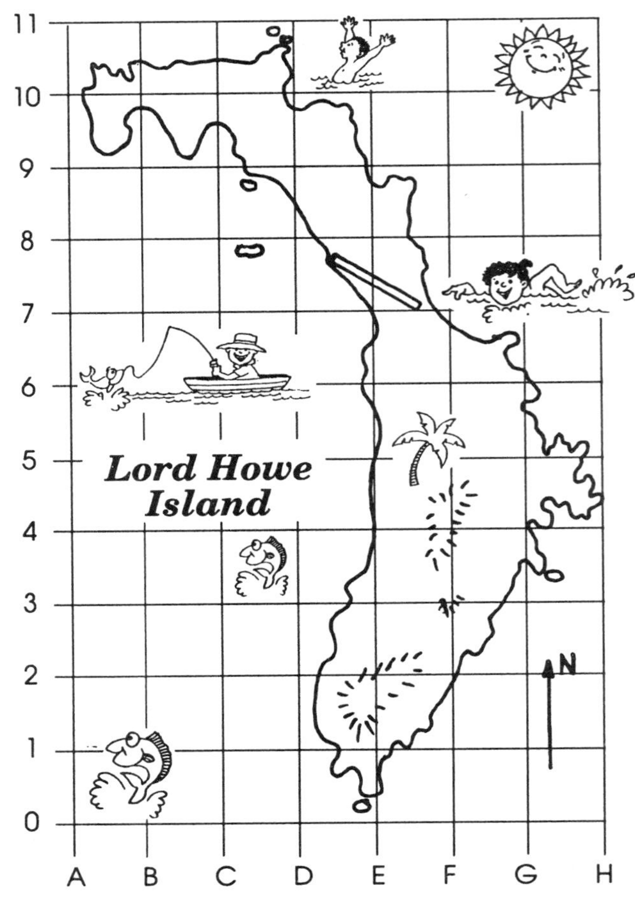

22. What else can you find out about Lord Howe Island?

____

____

____

____

____

____

Find three small boxes and work out the volume of each in **cm³**. Draw the boxes and show the length of each side in **centimetres.**

1.

_______ cm^3

2.

_______ cm^3

3.

_______ cm^3

4. Make a **prism** using eight square centimetre cubes. What is its volume? _______

5. Rearrange the 8 cubes into four new shapes and draw them here.

(a) (b)

(c) (d)

6. Draw the shapes in spaces on the grid.

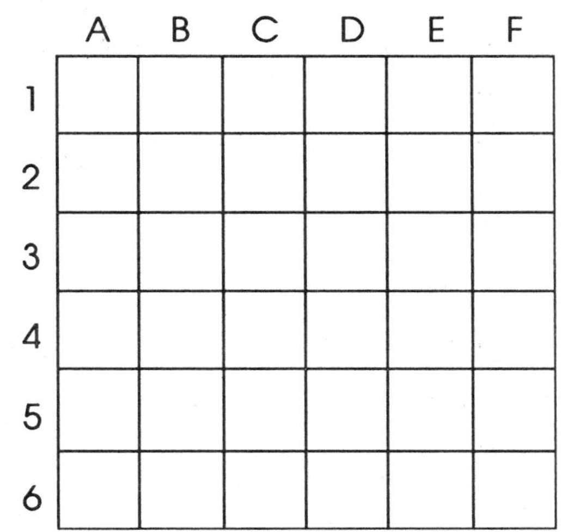

(a) Draw a circle in D3
(b) Draw an X in F6
(c) Draw a diamond in C5
(d) Shade B3 and E2
(e) Draw a triangle in A4

7. $54 \div 9 =$ _______ 8. $48 \div 8 =$ _______

9. $45 \div 9 =$ _______ 10. $42 \div 6 =$ _______

11. $63 \div 7 =$ _______ 12. $96 \div 8 =$ _______

Write the remainders only for these activities.

13. $7\overline{)50}$ 14. $9\overline{)74}$ 15. $8\overline{)66}$

16. $6\overline{)58}$ 17. $7\overline{)69}$ 18. $11\overline{)82}$

19. Share 28 mints among 6. How many each? Any left over?

_______ mints _______ left over

20. Divide 48 cubes among 5.

(a) How many each? _______

(b) How many left over? _______

1. $2\overline{)21}$ r

2. $7\overline{)76}$ r

3. $9\overline{)84}$ r

4. $4\overline{)37}$ r

5. $3\overline{)29}$ r

6. $6\overline{)57}$ r

7. $5\overline{)47}$ r

8. $8\overline{)79}$ r

9. $10\overline{)96}$ r

10. Fill in the **division** wheel. The outside spaces are for **remainders.**

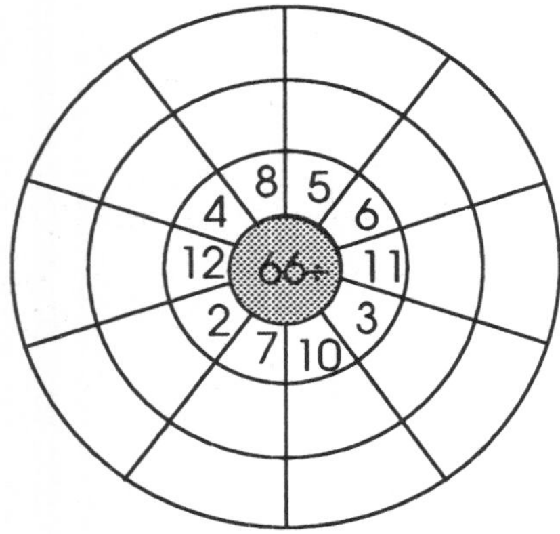

11. Alison has a box of 48 chocolates which she passes around to 9 guests so they each have the same number. Alison has the few that are left. How many? ______

12. A 93cm piece of wood is cut into 8cm lengths. How many lengths? How much left over?

______ lengths ______ cm left over

13. Divide 87 matches among 7. How many each? How many left over?

______ matches ______ left over.

14. Sixty-nine children are to have swimming lessons. There are no more than 8 to a group. How many teachers needed for the children? ______

15. This is a plan of a park. Add letters and numbers to the co-ordinates, then give the position of each feature.

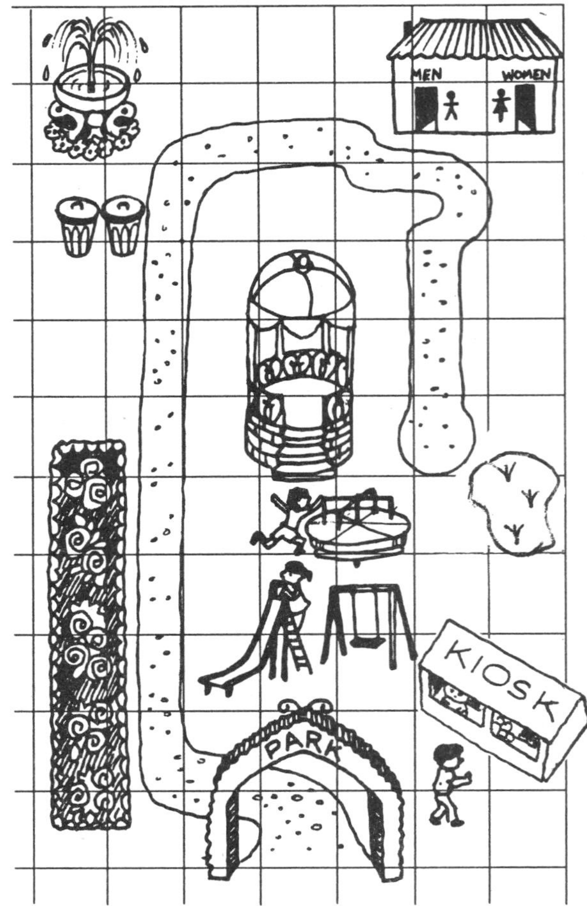

(a) Fountain ______ (b) Kiosk ______

(c) Flowerbed ______ (d) Litter bins ______

(e) Bandstand ______ (f) Duck pond ______

(g) Toilets ______ (h) Entrance ______

(i) Slide ______ (j) Swing ______

16. Give directions for walking from the kiosk to the fountain.

______

______

______

Measure the weight of these objects in **grams**.

1. 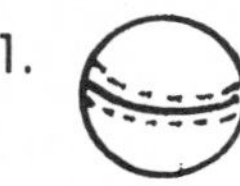 ________

2. 

____

3. 

____

4. 

____

5.  ________

6.  ________

Measure the weight of these heavier objects in **grams** or **kilograms** and **grams.**

7. 

____

8.  ________

9.  ________

10. 

____

Write these **weights** in the shortest possible way.

11. 2 350 grams ________

12. 4 kilograms 750 grams ________

13. 1 kilogram 70 grams ________

14. If you had some 30g weights and some 40g weights, what weights would you use to equal 140g?

____

15. Find out about the 'old' measure of weight, the ounce. How many grams are equal to one ounce?

____

16. 5) 27 r ___

17. 7) 59 r ___

18. 8) 52 r ___

19. 6) 64 r ___

20. 10) 77 r ___

21. 9) 50 r ___

22. 7) 61 r ___

23. 8) 70 r ___

24. 9) 93 r ___

25. Fifty-nine taxis are to operate in 7 areas, with the same number of taxis in each area. How many taxis left over? ________

26. Ninety-six pigs placed equally in 9 pens. How many pigs to be placed elsewhere? ________

27. A radio station orders 53 CDs to play in equal numbers in 8 programmes. How many should they have ordered for this? ________

28. There are 49 lines of poetry to be read by 8 children. Suggest how many children **should** have been selected. ________

29. Find the weight of each object

(a) an empty drinking glass ________

(b) pair of large scissors ________

(c) portable tape recorder ________

Write these weights the short way.

30. 1 756 grams ________

31. 95 grams ________

32. 820 grams ________

33. 8 grams ________

Unit 19

Write the shaded parts of these shapes as **fractions.**

1. 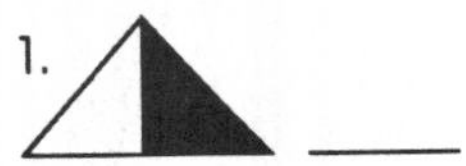 ____

2. ____

3. 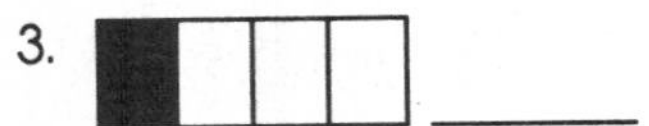 ____

4.  ____

5.  ____

6.  ____

7. 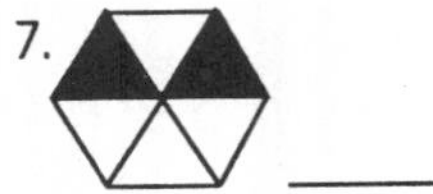 ____

8.  ____

9. 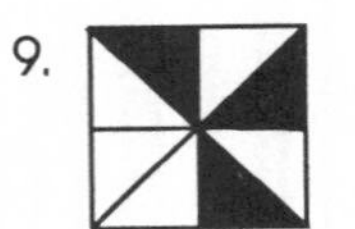 ____

10.  ____

Write the shaded items as a **fraction** of the total.

11.  ____

12. 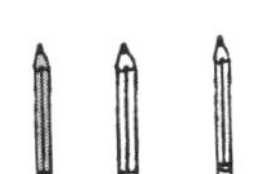 ____

13. 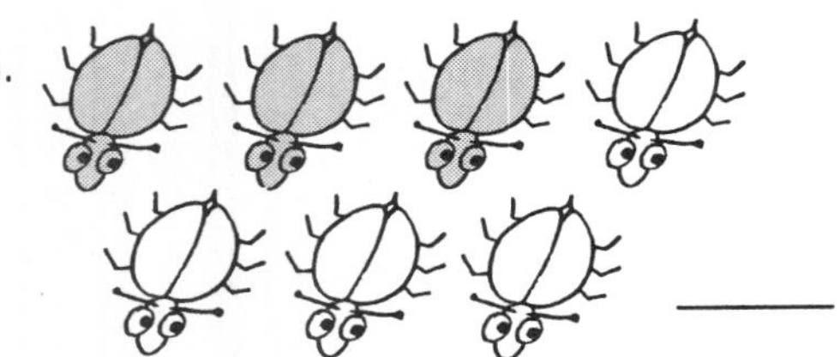 ____

14. 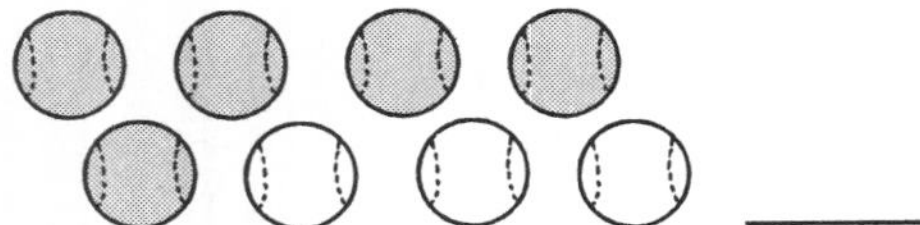 ____

15.  ____

16. 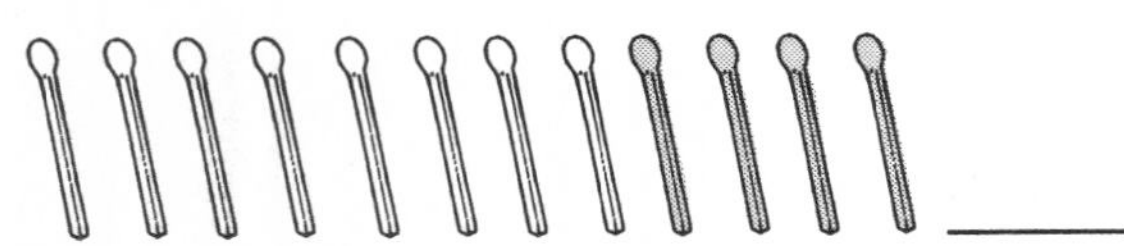 ____

17. List some appliances that measure temperature **in some way.**

____

____

____

____

____

____

18. Here are noon **temperatures** taken over one hot week in summer. Write the temperatures below.

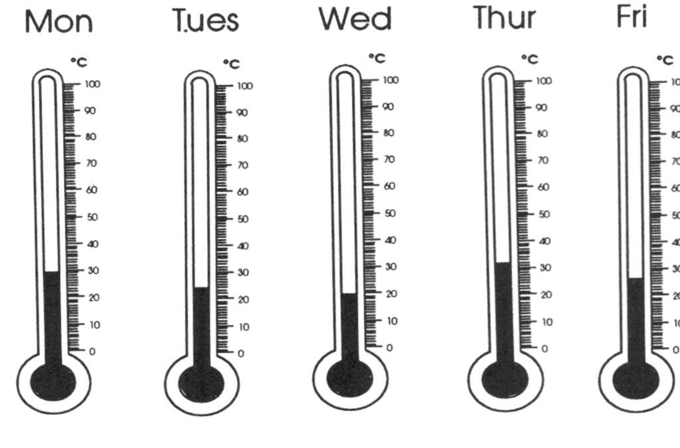

____ ____ ____ ____ ____

19. On a piece of paper, draw a graph of these **temperatures.**

Write the **differences** between these temperatures.

20. 47°C and 9°C ____

21. 245°C and 113°C ____

22. 4°C and 38°C ____

23. 149°C and 301°C ____

24. Can you have temperatures lower than the freezing point of water? ____

25. Measure your body **temperature.** ____

26. How hot is the sun's surface? ____

27. What does a clinical **thermometer** measure? ____

LEAP AHEAD

with

MATHS

Answers
Book 6

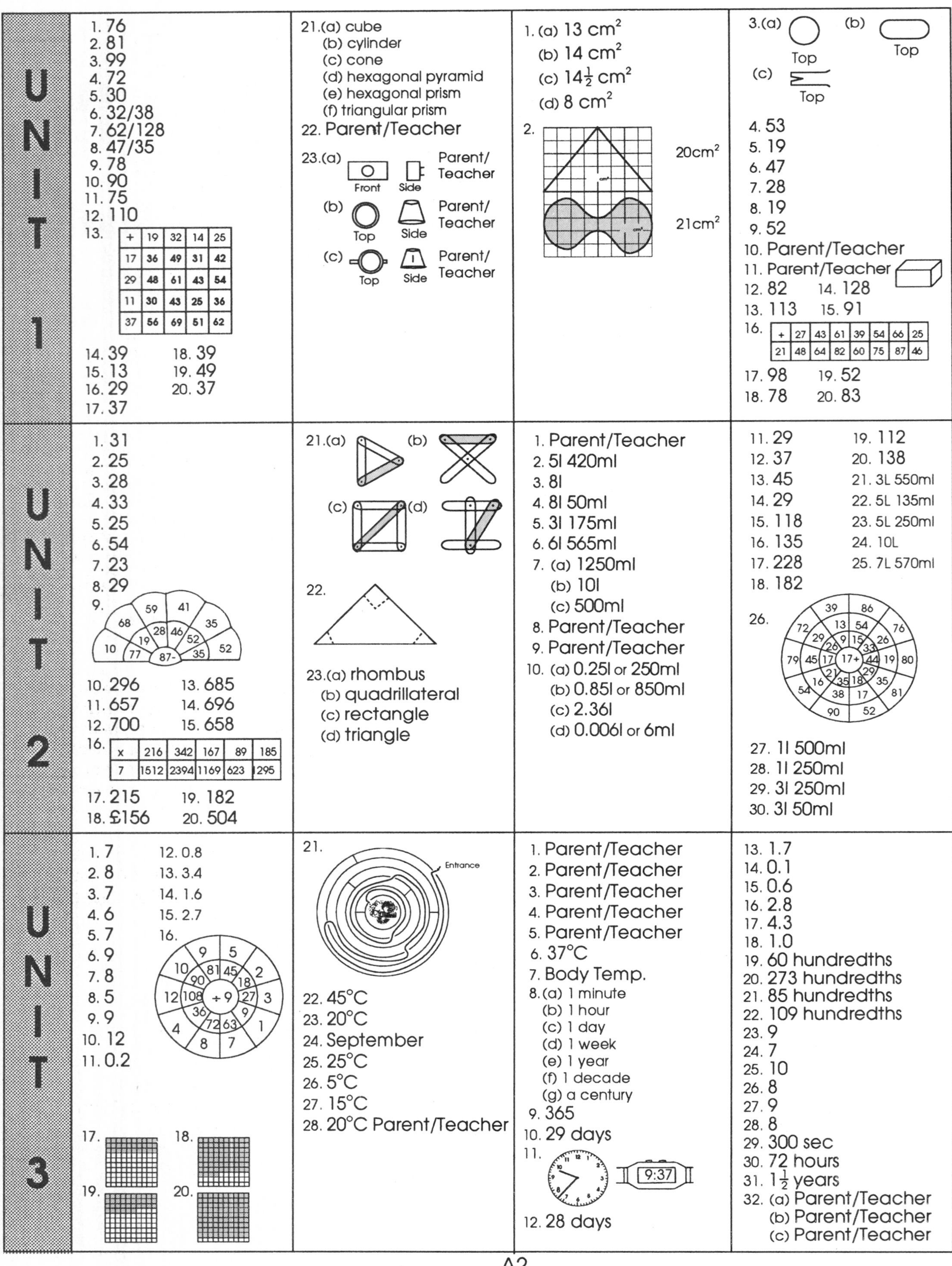

UNIT 1

1. 76
2. 81
3. 99
4. 72
5. 30
6. 32/38
7. 62/128
8. 47/35
9. 78
10. 90
11. 75
12. 110
13.

+	19	32	14	25
17	36	49	31	42
29	48	61	43	54
11	30	43	25	36
37	56	69	51	62

14. 39
15. 13
16. 29
17. 37
18. 39
19. 49
20. 37

21. (a) cube
(b) cylinder
(c) cone
(d) hexagonal pyramid
(e) hexagonal prism
(f) triangular prism
22. Parent/Teacher
23. (a) Front Side Parent/Teacher
(b) Top Side Parent/Teacher
(c) Top Side Parent/Teacher

1. (a) 13 cm^2
(b) 14 cm^2
(c) $14\frac{1}{2}$ cm^2
(d) 8 cm^2
2. 20cm^2
21cm^2

3. (a) Top (b) Top
(c) Top
4. 53
5. 19
6. 47
7. 28
8. 19
9. 52
10. Parent/Teacher
11. Parent/Teacher
12. 82
13. 113
14. 128
15. 91
16.

+	27	43	61	39	54	66	25
21	48	64	82	60	75	87	46

17. 98
18. 78
19. 52
20. 83

UNIT 2

1. 31
2. 25
3. 28
4. 33
5. 25
6. 54
7. 23
8. 29
9. 59, 41, 68, 35, 28, 46, 19, 52, 10, 77, 87-, 35, 52
10. 296
11. 657
12. 700
13. 685
14. 696
15. 658
16.

x	216	342	167	89	185
7	1512	2394	1169	623	1295

17. 215
18. £156
19. 182
20. 504

21. (a) (b) (c) (d)
22.
23. (a) rhombus
(b) quadrilateral
(c) rectangle
(d) triangle

1. Parent/Teacher
2. 5l 420ml
3. 8l
4. 8l 50ml
5. 3l 175ml
6. 6l 565ml
7. (a) 1250ml
(b) 10l
(c) 500ml
8. Parent/Teacher
9. Parent/Teacher
10. (a) 0.25l or 250ml
(b) 0.85l or 850ml
(c) 2.36l
(d) 0.006l or 6ml

11. 29
12. 37
13. 45
14. 29
15. 118
16. 135
17. 228
18. 182
19. 112
20. 138
21. 3L 550ml
22. 5L 135ml
23. 5L 250ml
24. 10L
25. 7L 570ml
26. 17+: 39, 86, 72, 13, 54, 76, 29, 9, 15, 26, 26, 33, 79, 45, 17, 44, 19, 80, 21, 29, 16, 35, 18, 35, 54, 38, 17, 81, 90, 52
27. 1l 500ml
28. 1l 250ml
29. 3l 250ml
30. 3l 50ml

UNIT 3

1. 7
2. 8
3. 7
4. 6
5. 7
6. 9
7. 8
8. 5
9. 9
10. 12
11. 0.2
12. 0.8
13. 3.4
14. 1.6
15. 2.7
16. ÷9: 9, 5, 10, 81, 45, 2, 90, 18, 12, 108, 27, 3, 36, 9, 72, 63, 4, 1, 8, 7
17.
18.
19.
20.

21. Entrance
22. 45°C
23. 20°C
24. September
25. 25°C
26. 5°C
27. 15°C
28. 20°C Parent/Teacher

1. Parent/Teacher
2. Parent/Teacher
3. Parent/Teacher
4. Parent/Teacher
5. Parent/Teacher
6. 37°C
7. Body Temp.
8. (a) 1 minute
(b) 1 hour
(c) 1 day
(d) 1 week
(e) 1 year
(f) 1 decade
(g) a century
9. 365
10. 29 days
11. 9:37
12. 28 days

13. 1.7
14. 0.1
15. 0.6
16. 2.8
17. 4.3
18. 1.0
19. 60 hundredths
20. 273 hundredths
21. 85 hundredths
22. 109 hundredths
23. 9
24. 7
25. 10
26. 8
27. 9
28. 8
29. 300 sec
30. 72 hours
31. $1\frac{1}{2}$ years
32. (a) Parent/Teacher
(b) Parent/Teacher
(c) Parent/Teacher

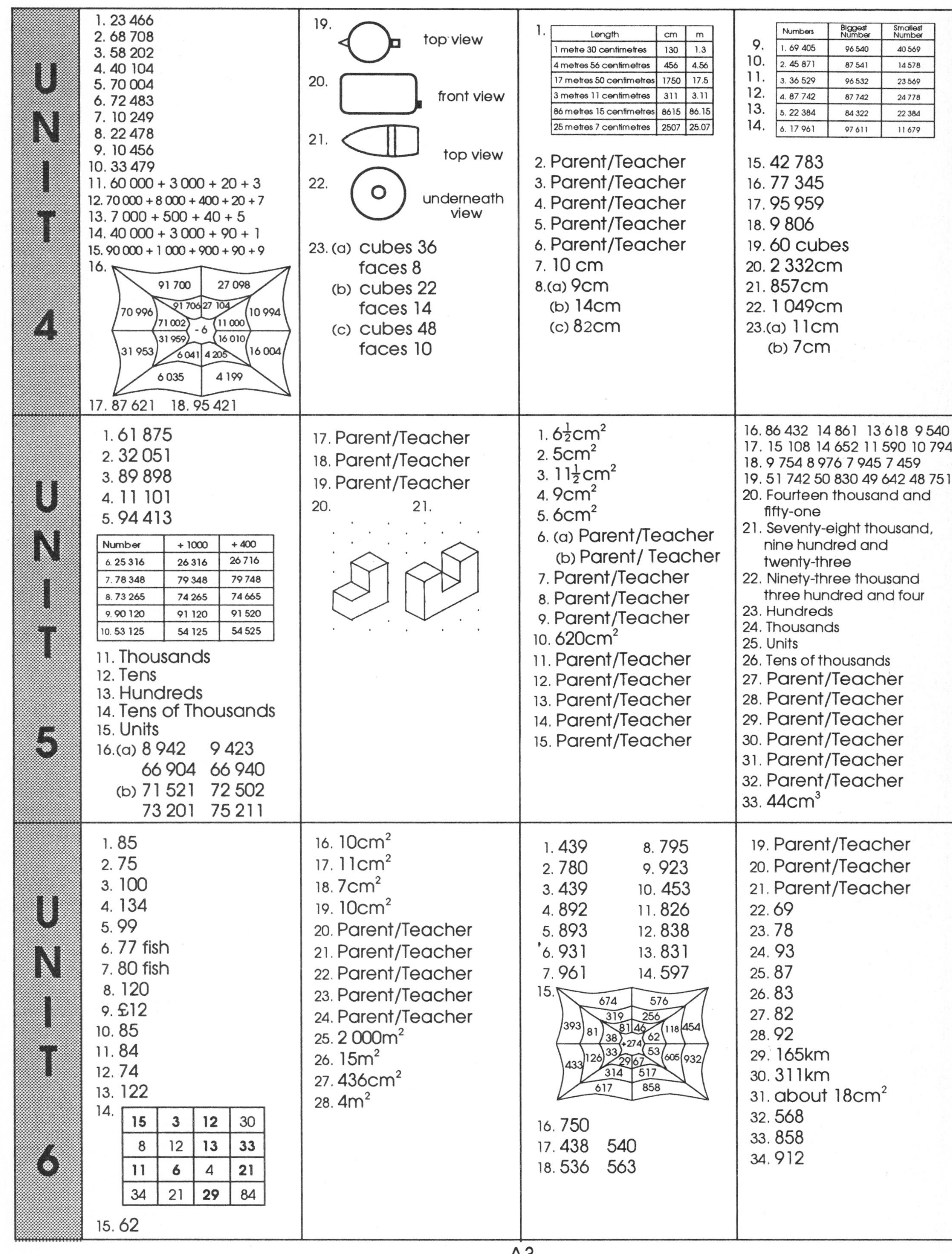

UNIT 4

1. 23 466
2. 68 708
3. 58 202
4. 40 104
5. 70 004
6. 72 483
7. 10 249
8. 22 478
9. 10 456
10. 33 479
11. 60 000 + 3 000 + 20 + 3
12. 70 000 + 8 000 + 400 + 20 + 7
13. 7 000 + 500 + 40 + 5
14. 40 000 + 3 000 + 90 + 1
15. 90 000 + 1 000 + 900 + 90 + 9
16.

17. 87 621   18. 95 421

19. top view
20. front view
21. top view
22. underneath view
23. (a) cubes 36 faces 8
    (b) cubes 22 faces 14
    (c) cubes 48 faces 10

1.

Length	cm	m
1 metre 30 centimetres	130	1.3
4 metres 56 centimetres	456	4.56
17 metres 50 centimetres	1750	17.5
3 metres 11 centimetres	311	3.11
86 metres 15 centimetres	8615	86.15
25 metres 7 centimetres	2507	25.07

2. Parent/Teacher
3. Parent/Teacher
4. Parent/Teacher
5. Parent/Teacher
6. Parent/Teacher
7. 10 cm
8. (a) 9cm
   (b) 14cm
   (c) 82cm

	Numbers	Biggest Number	Smallest Number
9.	1. 69 405	96 540	40 569
10.	2. 45 871	87 541	14 578
11.	3. 36 529	96 532	23 569
12.	4. 87 742	87 742	24 778
13.	5. 22 384	84 322	22 384
14.	6. 17 961	97 611	11 679

15. 42 783
16. 77 345
17. 95 959
18. 9 806
19. 60 cubes
20. 2 332cm
21. 857cm
22. 1 049cm
23. (a) 11cm
    (b) 7cm

UNIT 5

1. 61 875
2. 32 051
3. 89 898
4. 11 101
5. 94 413

Number	+ 1000	+ 400
6. 25 316	26 316	26 716
7. 78 348	79 348	79 748
8. 73 265	74 265	74 665
9. 90 120	91 120	91 520
10. 53 125	54 125	54 525

11. Thousands
12. Tens
13. Hundreds
14. Tens of Thousands
15. Units
16. (a) 8 942   9 423
    66 904   66 940
    (b) 71 521   72 502
    73 201   75 211

17. Parent/Teacher
18. Parent/Teacher
19. Parent/Teacher
20.   21.

1. $6\frac{1}{2}cm^2$
2. $5cm^2$
3. $11\frac{1}{2}cm^2$
4. $9cm^2$
5. $6cm^2$
6. (a) Parent/Teacher
   (b) Parent/ Teacher
7. Parent/Teacher
8. Parent/Teacher
9. Parent/Teacher
10. $620cm^2$
11. Parent/Teacher
12. Parent/Teacher
13. Parent/Teacher
14. Parent/Teacher
15. Parent/Teacher

16. 86 432 14 861 13 618 9 540
17. 15 108 14 652 11 590 10 794
18. 9 754 8 976 7 945 7 459
19. 51 742 50 830 49 642 48 751
20. Fourteen thousand and fifty-one
21. Seventy-eight thousand, nine hundred and twenty-three
22. Ninety-three thousand three hundred and four
23. Hundreds
24. Thousands
25. Units
26. Tens of thousands
27. Parent/Teacher
28. Parent/Teacher
29. Parent/Teacher
30. Parent/Teacher
31. Parent/Teacher
32. Parent/Teacher
33. $44cm^3$

UNIT 6

1. 85
2. 75
3. 100
4. 134
5. 99
6. 77 fish
7. 80 fish
8. 120
9. £12
10. 85
11. 84
12. 74
13. 122
14.

15	3	**12**	30
8	12	**13**	**33**
11	**6**	4	**21**
34	21	**29**	84

15. 62

16. $10cm^2$
17. $11cm^2$
18. $7cm^2$
19. $10cm^2$
20. Parent/Teacher
21. Parent/Teacher
22. Parent/Teacher
23. Parent/Teacher
24. Parent/Teacher
25. $2\,000m^2$
26. $15m^2$
27. $436cm^2$
28. $4m^2$

1. 439
2. 780
3. 439
4. 892
5. 893
6. 931
7. 961
8. 795
9. 923
10. 453
11. 826
12. 838
13. 831
14. 597
15.

16. 750
17. 438   540
18. 536   563

19. Parent/Teacher
20. Parent/Teacher
21. Parent/Teacher
22. 69
23. 78
24. 93
25. 87
26. 83
27. 82
28. 92
29. 165km
30. 311km
31. about $18cm^2$
32. 568
33. 858
34. 912

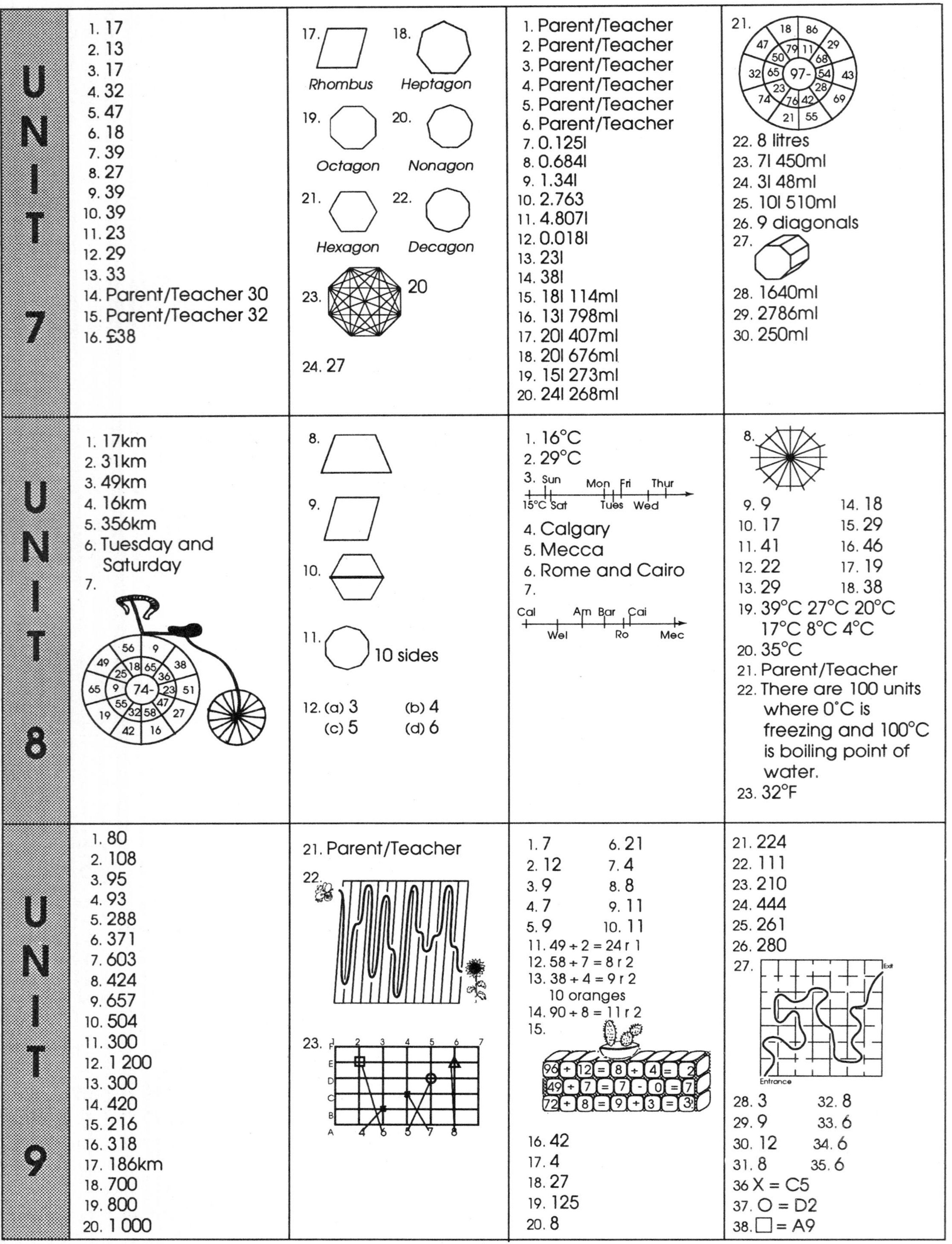

UNIT 7

1. 17
2. 13
3. 17
4. 32
5. 47
6. 18
7. 39
8. 27
9. 39
10. 39
11. 23
12. 29
13. 33
14. Parent/Teacher 30
15. Parent/Teacher 32
16. £38

17. Rhombus
18. Heptagon
19. Octagon
20. Nonagon
21. Hexagon
22. Decagon
23. 20
24. 27

1. Parent/Teacher
2. Parent/Teacher
3. Parent/Teacher
4. Parent/Teacher
5. Parent/Teacher
6. Parent/Teacher
7. 0.125l
8. 0.684l
9. 1.34l
10. 2.763
11. 4.807l
12. 0.018l
13. 23l
14. 38l
15. 18l 114ml
16. 13l 798ml
17. 20l 407ml
18. 20l 676ml
19. 15l 273ml
20. 24l 268ml

21.

22. 8 litres
23. 7l 450ml
24. 3l 48ml
25. 10l 510ml
26. 9 diagonals
27.
28. 1640ml
29. 2786ml
30. 250ml

UNIT 8

1. 17km
2. 31km
3. 49km
4. 16km
5. 356km
6. Tuesday and Saturday
7.

8.
9.
10.
11. 10 sides
12. (a) 3 (b) 4 (c) 5 (d) 6

1. 16°C
2. 29°C
3.

4. Calgary
5. Mecca
6. Rome and Cairo
7.

8.
9. 9
10. 17
11. 41
12. 22
13. 29
14. 18
15. 29
16. 46
17. 19
18. 38
19. 39°C 27°C 20°C 17°C 8°C 4°C
20. 35°C
21. Parent/Teacher
22. There are 100 units where 0°C is freezing and 100°C is boiling point of water.
23. 32°F

UNIT 9

1. 80
2. 108
3. 95
4. 93
5. 288
6. 371
7. 603
8. 424
9. 657
10. 504
11. 300
12. 1 200
13. 300
14. 420
15. 216
16. 318
17. 186km
18. 700
19. 800
20. 1 000

21. Parent/Teacher
22.
23.

1. 7
2. 12
3. 9
4. 7
5. 9
6. 21
7. 4
8. 8
9. 11
10. 11
11. 49 ÷ 2 = 24 r 1
12. 58 ÷ 7 = 8 r 2
13. 38 ÷ 4 = 9 r 2 10 oranges
14. 90 ÷ 8 = 11 r 2
15.

16. 42
17. 4
18. 27
19. 125
20. 8

21. 224
22. 111
23. 210
24. 444
25. 261
26. 280
27.

28. 3
29. 9
30. 12
31. 8
32. 8
33. 6
34. 6
35. 6
36. X = C5
37. O = D2
38. □ = A9

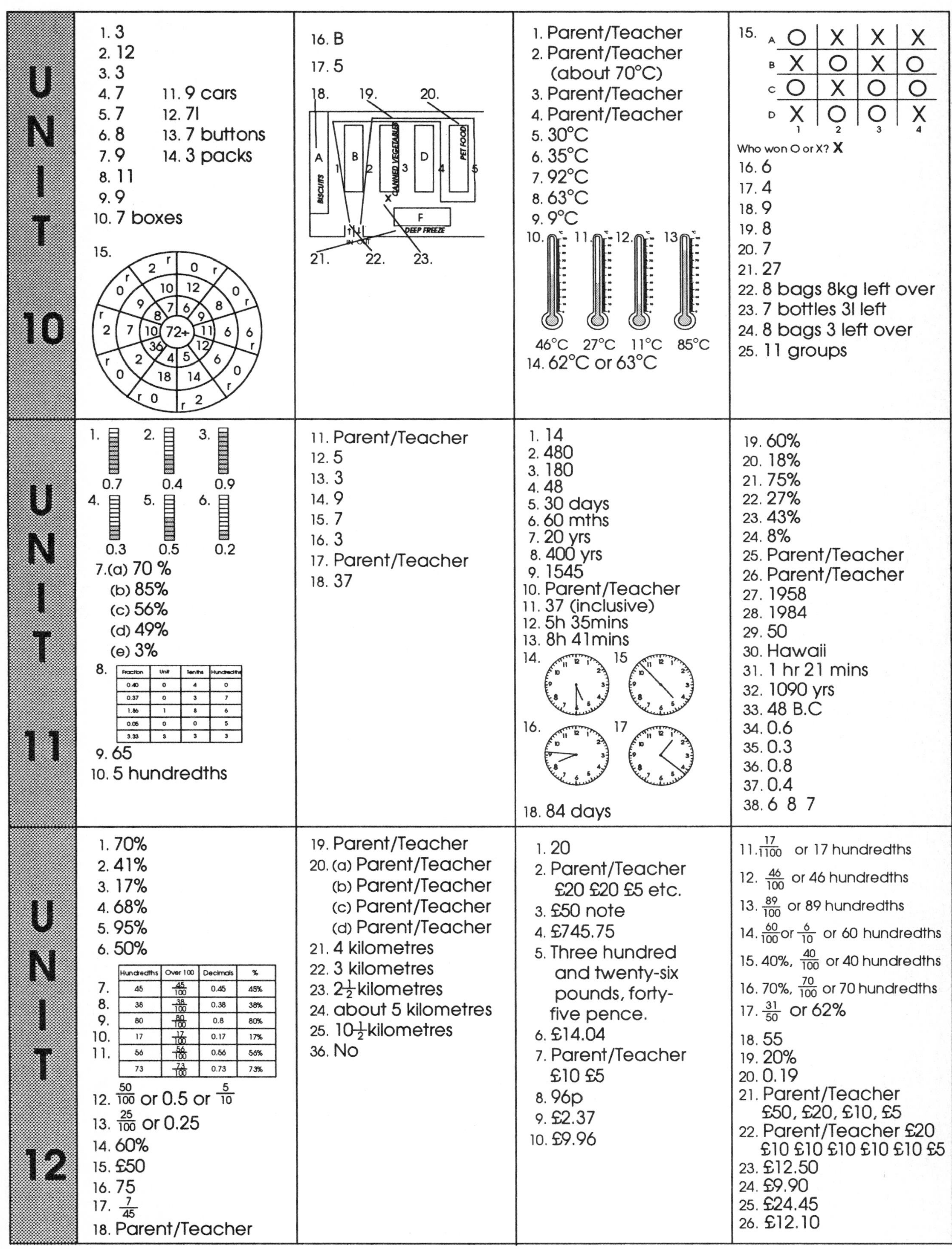

UNIT 10

1. 3
2. 12
3. 3
4. 7
5. 7
6. 8
7. 9
8. 11
9. 9
10. 7 boxes
11. 9 cars
12. 7l
13. 7 buttons
14. 3 packs
15.

16. B
17. 5
18. 19. 20.

21. 22. 23.

1. Parent/Teacher
2. Parent/Teacher (about 70°C)
3. Parent/Teacher
4. Parent/Teacher
5. 30°C
6. 35°C
7. 92°C
8. 63°C
9. 9°C

10. 46°C 11. 27°C 12. 11°C 13. 85°C

14. 62°C or 63°C

15.

	1	2	3	4
A	O	X	X	X
B	X	O	X	O
C	O	X	O	O
D	X	O	O	X

Who won O or X? **X**

16. 6
17. 4
18. 9
19. 8
20. 7
21. 27
22. 8 bags 8kg left over
23. 7 bottles 3l left
24. 8 bags 3 left over
25. 11 groups

UNIT 11

1. 0.7
2. 0.4
3. 0.9
4. 0.3
5. 0.5
6. 0.2

7.(a) 70 %
(b) 85%
(c) 56%
(d) 49%
(e) 3%

8.

Fraction	Unit	Tenths	Hundredths
0.40	0	4	0
0.37	0	3	7
1.86	1	8	6
0.05	0	0	5
3.33	3	3	3

9. 65
10. 5 hundredths
11. Parent/Teacher
12. 5
13. 3
14. 9
15. 7
16. 3
17. Parent/Teacher
18. 37

1. 14
2. 480
3. 180
4. 48
5. 30 days
6. 60 mths
7. 20 yrs
8. 400 yrs
9. 1545
10. Parent/Teacher
11. 37 (inclusive)
12. 5h 35mins
13. 8h 41mins
14. 15
16. 17
18. 84 days

19. 60%
20. 18%
21. 75%
22. 27%
23. 43%
24. 8%
25. Parent/Teacher
26. Parent/Teacher
27. 1958
28. 1984
29. 50
30. Hawaii
31. 1 hr 21 mins
32. 1090 yrs
33. 48 B.C
34. 0.6
35. 0.3
36. 0.8
37. 0.4
38. 6 8 7

UNIT 12

1. 70%
2. 41%
3. 17%
4. 68%
5. 95%
6. 50%

	Hundredths	Over 100	Decimals	%
7.	45	$\frac{45}{100}$	0.45	45%
8.	38	$\frac{38}{100}$	0.38	38%
9.	80	$\frac{80}{100}$	0.8	80%
10.	17	$\frac{17}{100}$	0.17	17%
11.	56	$\frac{56}{100}$	0.56	56%
	73	$\frac{73}{100}$	0.73	73%

12. $\frac{50}{100}$ or 0.5 or $\frac{5}{10}$
13. $\frac{25}{100}$ or 0.25
14. 60%
15. £50
16. 75
17. $\frac{7}{45}$
18. Parent/Teacher
19. Parent/Teacher
20. (a) Parent/Teacher
(b) Parent/Teacher
(c) Parent/Teacher
(d) Parent/Teacher
21. 4 kilometres
22. 3 kilometres
23. $2\frac{1}{2}$ kilometres
24. about 5 kilometres
25. $10\frac{1}{2}$ kilometres
36. No

1. 20
2. Parent/Teacher £20 £20 £5 etc.
3. £50 note
4. £745.75
5. Three hundred and twenty-six pounds, forty-five pence.
6. £14.04
7. Parent/Teacher £10 £5
8. 96p
9. £2.37
10. £9.96

11. $\frac{17}{1100}$ or 17 hundredths
12. $\frac{46}{100}$ or 46 hundredths
13. $\frac{89}{100}$ or 89 hundredths
14. $\frac{60}{100}$ or $\frac{6}{10}$ or 60 hundredths
15. 40%, $\frac{40}{100}$ or 40 hundredths
16. 70%, $\frac{70}{100}$ or 70 hundredths
17. $\frac{31}{50}$ or 62%
18. 55
19. 20%
20. 0.19
21. Parent/Teacher £50, £20, £10, £5
22. Parent/Teacher £20 £10 £10 £10 £10 £10 £5
23. £12.50
24. £9.90
25. £24.45
26. £12.10

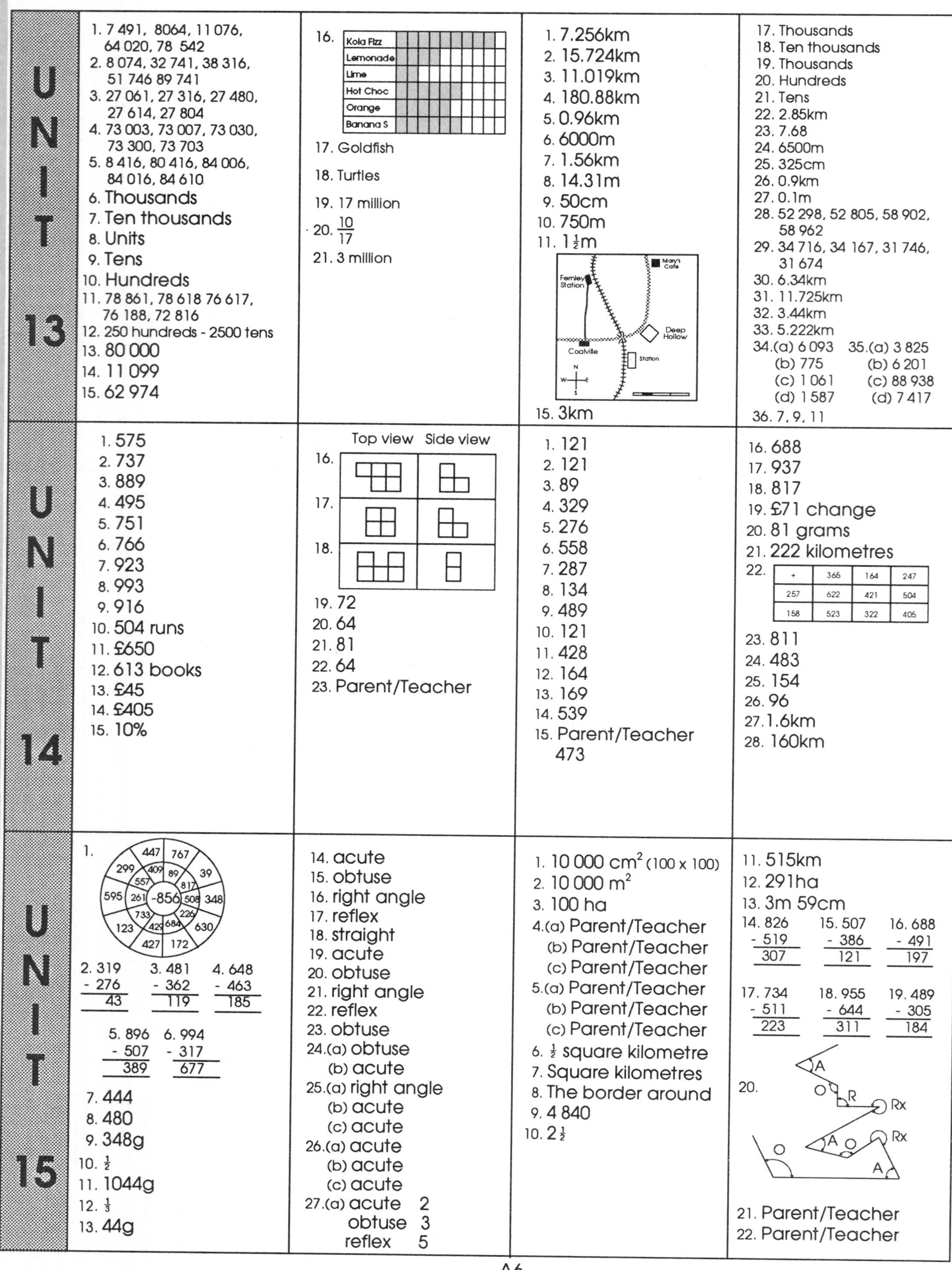

UNIT 13

1. 7 491, 8064, 11 076, 64 020, 78 542
2. 8 074, 32 741, 38 316, 51 746 89 741
3. 27 061, 27 316, 27 480, 27 614, 27 804
4. 73 003, 73 007, 73 030, 73 300, 73 703
5. 8 416, 80 416, 84 006, 84 016, 84 610
6. Thousands
7. Ten thousands
8. Units
9. Tens
10. Hundreds
11. 78 861, 78 618 76 617, 76 188, 72 816
12. 250 hundreds - 2500 tens
13. 80 000
14. 11 099
15. 62 974

16\.

17. Goldfish
18. Turtles
19. 17 million
20. $\frac{10}{17}$
21. 3 million

1. 7.256km
2. 15.724km
3. 11.019km
4. 180.88km
5. 0.96km
6. 6000m
7. 1.56km
8. 14.31m
9. 50cm
10. 750m
11. $1\frac{1}{2}$m

15. 3km

17. Thousands
18. Ten thousands
19. Thousands
20. Hundreds
21. Tens
22. 2.85km
23. 7.68
24. 6500m
25. 325cm
26. 0.9km
27. 0.1m
28. 52 298, 52 805, 58 902, 58 962
29. 34 716, 34 167, 31 746, 31 674
30. 6.34km
31. 11.725km
32. 3.44km
33. 5.222km
34. (a) 6 093 (b) 775 (c) 1 061 (d) 1 587
35. (a) 3 825 (b) 6 201 (c) 88 938 (d) 7 417
36. 7, 9, 11

UNIT 14

1. 575
2. 737
3. 889
4. 495
5. 751
6. 766
7. 923
8. 993
9. 916
10. 504 runs
11. £650
12. 613 books
13. £45
14. £405
15. 10%

Top view Side view

16\.
17\.
18\.

19. 72
20. 64
21. 81
22. 64
23. Parent/Teacher

1. 121
2. 121
3. 89
4. 329
5. 276
6. 558
7. 287
8. 134
9. 489
10. 121
11. 428
12. 164
13. 169
14. 539
15. Parent/Teacher 473

16. 688
17. 937
18. 817
19. £71 change
20. 81 grams
21. 222 kilometres
22\.

+	365	164	247
257	622	421	504
158	523	322	405

23. 811
24. 483
25. 154
26. 96
27. 1.6km
28. 160km

UNIT 15

1\.

2. 319 - 276 = 43
3. 481 - 362 = 119
4. 648 - 463 = 185
5. 896 - 507 = 389
6. 994 - 317 = 677
7. 444
8. 480
9. 348g
10. $\frac{1}{2}$
11. 1044g
12. $\frac{1}{3}$
13. 44g

14. acute
15. obtuse
16. right angle
17. reflex
18. straight
19. acute
20. obtuse
21. right angle
22. reflex
23. obtuse
24. (a) obtuse (b) acute
25. (a) right angle (b) acute (c) acute
26. (a) acute (b) acute (c) acute
27. (a) acute 2, obtuse 3, reflex 5

1. 10 000 cm^2 (100 x 100)
2. 10 000 m^2
3. 100 ha
4. (a) Parent/Teacher (b) Parent/Teacher (c) Parent/Teacher
5. (a) Parent/Teacher (b) Parent/Teacher (c) Parent/Teacher
6. $\frac{1}{2}$ square kilometre
7. Square kilometres
8. The border around
9. 4 840
10. $2\frac{1}{2}$

11. 515km
12. 291ha
13. 3m 59cm
14. 826 - 519 = 307
15. 507 - 386 = 121
16. 688 - 491 = 197
17. 734 - 511 = 223
18. 955 - 644 = 311
19. 489 - 305 = 184
20\.

21. Parent/Teacher
22. Parent/Teacher

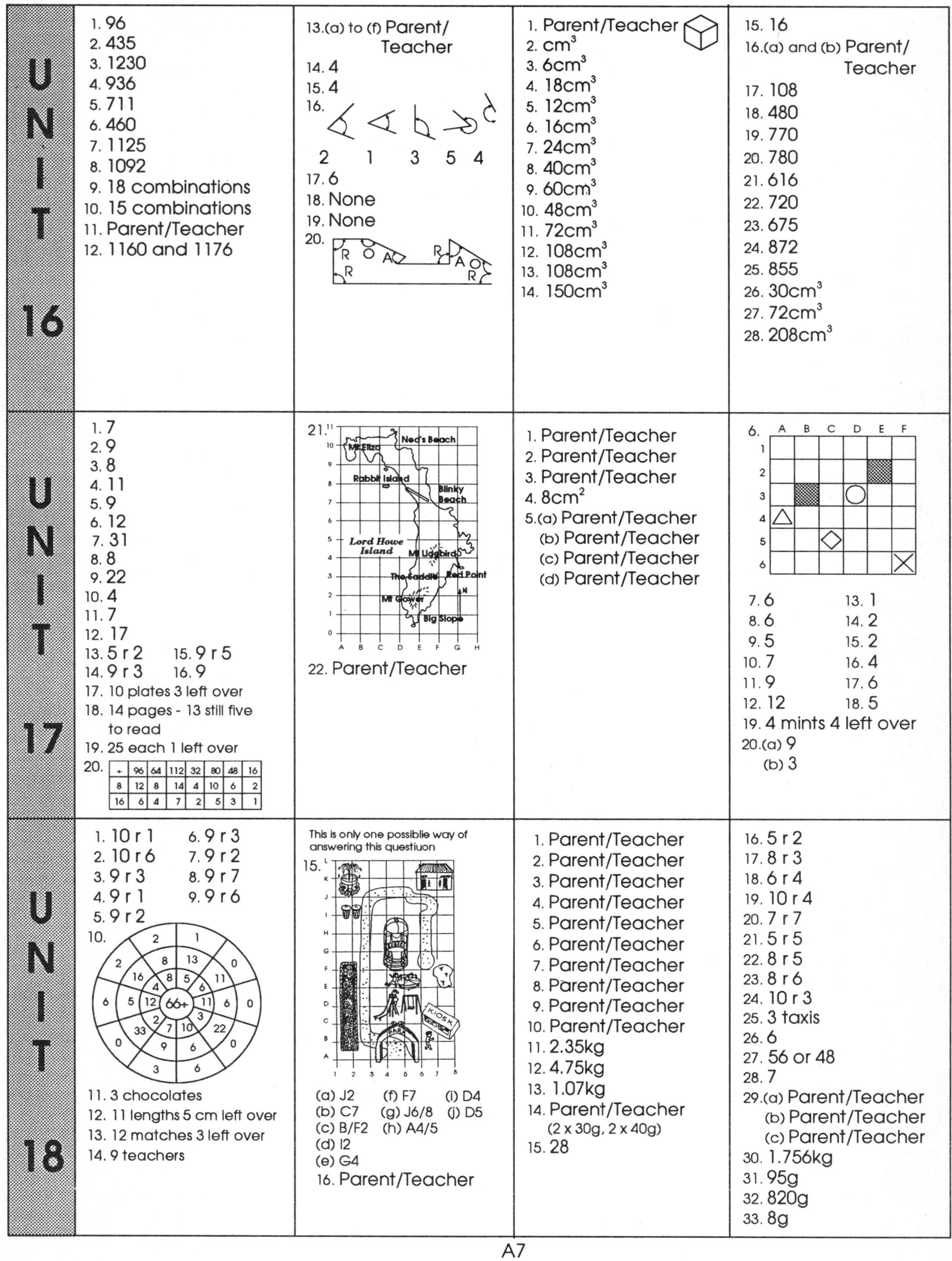

UNIT 16

1. 96
2. 435
3. 1230
4. 936
5. 711
6. 460
7. 1125
8. 1092
9. 18 combinations
10. 15 combinations
11. Parent/Teacher
12. 1160 and 1176

13.(a) to (f) Parent/Teacher
14. 4
15. 4
16. 2 1 3 5 4
17. 6
18. None
19. None
20.

1. Parent/Teacher
2. cm^3
3. $6cm^3$
4. $18cm^3$
5. $12cm^3$
6. $16cm^3$
7. $24cm^3$
8. $40cm^3$
9. $60cm^3$
10. $48cm^3$
11. $72cm^3$
12. $108cm^3$
13. $108cm^3$
14. $150cm^3$

15. 16
16.(a) and (b) Parent/Teacher
17. 108
18. 480
19. 770
20. 780
21. 616
22. 720
23. 675
24. 872
25. 855
26. $30cm^3$
27. $72cm^3$
28. $208cm^3$

UNIT 17

1. 7
2. 9
3. 8
4. 11
5. 9
6. 12
7. 31
8. 8
9. 22
10. 4
11. 7
12. 17
13. 5 r 2
14. 9 r 3
15. 9 r 5
16. 9
17. 10 plates 3 left over
18. 14 pages - 13 still five to read
19. 25 each 1 left over
20.

÷	96	64	112	32	80	48	16
8	12	8	14	4	10	6	2
16	6	4	7	2	5	3	1

21.

22. Parent/Teacher

1. Parent/Teacher
2. Parent/Teacher
3. Parent/Teacher
4. $8cm^2$
5.(a) Parent/Teacher
(b) Parent/Teacher
(c) Parent/Teacher
(d) Parent/Teacher

6.

7. 6
8. 6
9. 5
10. 7
11. 9
12. 12
13. 1
14. 2
15. 2
16. 4
17. 6
18. 5
19. 4 mints 4 left over
20.(a) 9
(b) 3

UNIT 18

1. 10 r 1
2. 10 r 6
3. 9 r 3
4. 9 r 1
5. 9 r 2
6. 9 r 3
7. 9 r 2
8. 9 r 7
9. 9 r 6
10.

11. 3 chocolates
12. 11 lengths 5 cm left over
13. 12 matches 3 left over
14. 9 teachers

This is only one possiblie way of answering this questiuon

15.

(a) J2
(b) C7
(c) B/F2
(d) I2
(e) G4
(f) F7
(g) J6/8
(h) A4/5
(i) D4
(j) D5

16. Parent/Teacher

1. Parent/Teacher
2. Parent/Teacher
3. Parent/Teacher
4. Parent/Teacher
5. Parent/Teacher
6. Parent/Teacher
7. Parent/Teacher
8. Parent/Teacher
9. Parent/Teacher
10. Parent/Teacher
11. 2.35kg
12. 4.75kg
13. 1.07kg
14. Parent/Teacher (2 x 30g, 2 x 40g)
15. 28

16. 5 r 2
17. 8 r 3
18. 6 r 4
19. 10 r 4
20. 7 r 7
21. 5 r 5
22. 8 r 5
23. 8 r 6
24. 10 r 3
25. 3 taxis
26. 6
27. 56 or 48
28. 7
29.(a) Parent/Teacher
(b) Parent/Teacher
(c) Parent/Teacher
30. 1.756kg
31. 95g
32. 820g
33. 8g

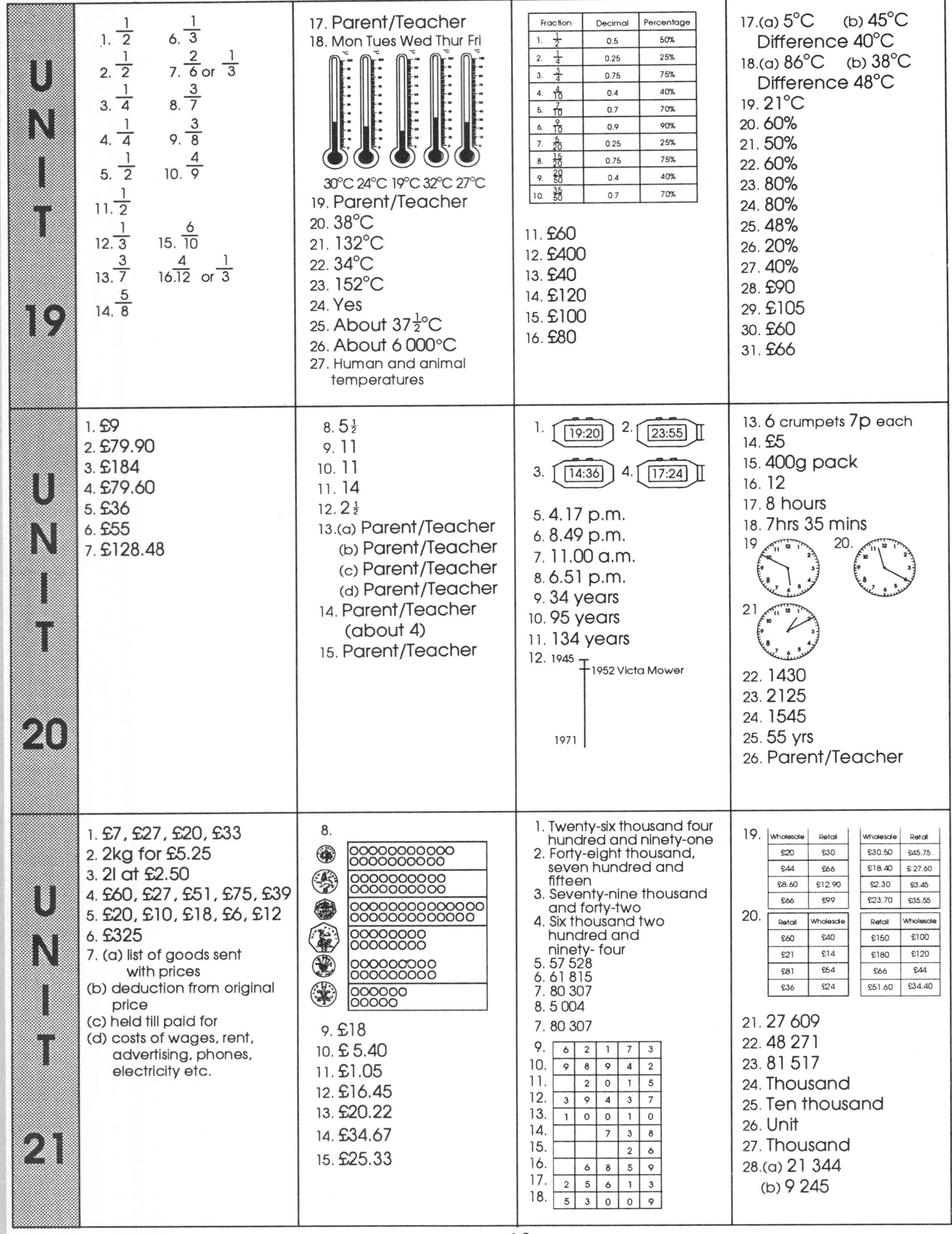

UNIT 19

1. $\frac{1}{2}$
2. $\frac{1}{2}$
3. $\frac{1}{4}$
4. $\frac{1}{4}$
5. $\frac{1}{2}$
6. $\frac{1}{3}$
7. $\frac{2}{6}$ or $\frac{1}{3}$
8. $\frac{3}{7}$
9. $\frac{3}{8}$
10. $\frac{4}{9}$
11. $\frac{1}{2}$
12. $\frac{1}{3}$
13. $\frac{3}{7}$
14. $\frac{5}{8}$
15. $\frac{6}{10}$
16. $\frac{4}{12}$ or $\frac{1}{3}$

17. Parent/Teacher
18. Mon Tues Wed Thur Fri

30°C 24°C 19°C 32°C 27°C

19. Parent/Teacher
20. 38°C
21. 132°C
22. 34°C
23. 152°C
24. Yes
25. About $37\frac{1}{2}$°C
26. About 6 000°C
27. Human and animal temperatures

Fraction	Decimal	Percentage
1. $\frac{1}{2}$	0.5	50%
2. $\frac{1}{4}$	0.25	25%
3. $\frac{3}{4}$	0.75	75%
4. $\frac{4}{10}$	0.4	40%
5. $\frac{7}{10}$	0.7	70%
6. $\frac{9}{10}$	0.9	90%
7. $\frac{5}{20}$	0.25	25%
8. $\frac{15}{20}$	0.75	75%
9. $\frac{20}{50}$	0.4	40%
10. $\frac{35}{50}$	0.7	70%

11. £60
12. £400
13. £40
14. £120
15. £100
16. £80

17. (a) 5°C (b) 45°C
Difference 40°C
18. (a) 86°C (b) 38°C
Difference 48°C
19. 21°C
20. 60%
21. 50%
22. 60%
23. 80%
24. 80%
25. 48%
26. 20%
27. 40%
28. £90
29. £105
30. £60
31. £66

UNIT 20

1. £9
2. £79.90
3. £184
4. £79.60
5. £36
6. £55
7. £128.48

8. $5\frac{1}{2}$
9. 11
10. 11
11. 14
12. $2\frac{1}{2}$
13. (a) Parent/Teacher
(b) Parent/Teacher
(c) Parent/Teacher
(d) Parent/Teacher
14. Parent/Teacher (about 4)
15. Parent/Teacher

1. 19:20
2. 23:55
3. 14:36
4. 17:24
5. 4.17 p.m.
6. 8.49 p.m.
7. 11.00 a.m.
8. 6.51 p.m.
9. 34 years
10. 95 years
11. 134 years
12. 1945 — 1952 Victa Mower — 1971

13. 6 crumpets 7p each
14. £5
15. 400g pack
16. 12
17. 8 hours
18. 7hrs 35 mins
19.
20.
21.
22. 1430
23. 2125
24. 1545
25. 55 yrs
26. Parent/Teacher

UNIT 21

1. £7, £27, £20, £33
2. 2kg for £5.25
3. 2l at £2.50
4. £60, £27, £51, £75, £39
5. £20, £10, £18, £6, £12
6. £325
7. (a) list of goods sent with prices
(b) deduction from original price
(c) held till paid for
(d) costs of wages, rent, advertising, phones, electricity etc.

8.

00000000000 0000000000
00000000000 0000000000
00000000000000 0000000000000
00000000 00000000
000000000 000000000
000000 00000

9. £18
10. £ 5.40
11. £1.05
12. £16.45
13. £20.22
14. £34.67
15. £25.33

1. Twenty-six thousand four hundred and ninety-one
2. Forty-eight thousand, seven hundred and fifteen
3. Seventy-nine thousand and forty-two
4. Six thousand two hundred and ninety- four
5. 57 528
6. 61 815
7. 80 307
8. 5 004

7. 80 307

9.	6	2	1	7	3
10.	9	8	9	4	2
11.		2	0	1	5
12.	3	9	4	3	7
13.	1	0	0	1	0
14.			7	3	8
15.				2	6
16.		6	8	5	9
17.	2	5	6	1	3
18.	5	3	0	0	9

19.

Wholesale	Retail
£20	£30
£44	£66
£8.60	£12.90
£66	£99

Wholesale	Retail
£30.50	£45.75
£18.40	£ 27.60
£2.30	£3.45
£23.70	£35.55

20.

Retail	Wholesale
£60	£40
£21	£14
£81	£54
£36	£24

Retail	Wholesale
£150	£100
£180	£120
£66	£44
£51.60	£34.40

21. 27 609
22. 48 271
23. 81 517
24. Thousand
25. Ten thousand
26. Unit
27. Thousand
28. (a) 21 344
(b) 9 245

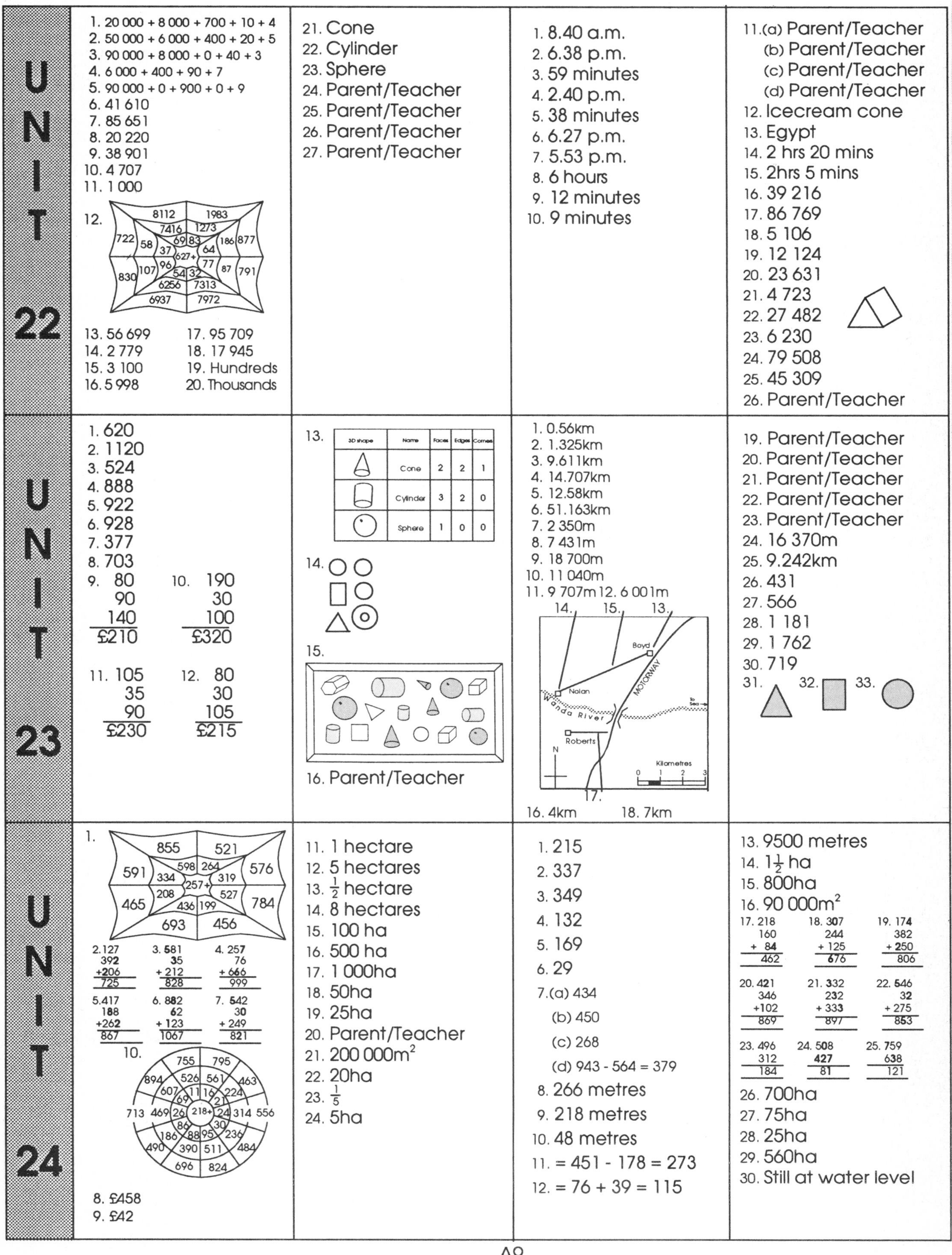

UNIT 22

1. 20 000 + 8 000 + 700 + 10 + 4
2. 50 000 + 6 000 + 400 + 20 + 5
3. 90 000 + 8 000 + 0 + 40 + 3
4. 6 000 + 400 + 90 + 7
5. 90 000 + 0 + 900 + 0 + 9
6. 41 610
7. 85 651
8. 20 220
9. 38 901
10. 4 707
11. 1 000
12.

13. 56 699
14. 2 779
15. 3 100
16. 5 998
17. 95 709
18. 17 945
19. Hundreds
20. Thousands
21. Cone
22. Cylinder
23. Sphere
24. Parent/Teacher
25. Parent/Teacher
26. Parent/Teacher
27. Parent/Teacher

1. 8.40 a.m.
2. 6.38 p.m.
3. 59 minutes
4. 2.40 p.m.
5. 38 minutes
6. 6.27 p.m.
7. 5.53 p.m.
8. 6 hours
9. 12 minutes
10. 9 minutes

11. (a) Parent/Teacher
    (b) Parent/Teacher
    (c) Parent/Teacher
    (d) Parent/Teacher
12. Icecream cone
13. Egypt
14. 2 hrs 20 mins
15. 2hrs 5 mins
16. 39 216
17. 86 769
18. 5 106
19. 12 124
20. 23 631
21. 4 723
22. 27 482
23. 6 230
24. 79 508
25. 45 309
26. Parent/Teacher

UNIT 23

1. 620
2. 1120
3. 524
4. 888
5. 922
6. 928
7. 377
8. 703
9. 80 / 90 / 140 / £210
10. 190 / 30 / 100 / £320
11. 105 / 35 / 90 / £230
12. 80 / 30 / 105 / £215

13.

3D shape	Name	Faces	Edges	Corners
	Cone	2	2	1
	Cylinder	3	2	0
	Sphere	1	0	0

14.

15.

16. Parent/Teacher

1. 0.56km
2. 1.325km
3. 9.611km
4. 14.707km
5. 12.58km
6. 51.163km
7. 2 350m
8. 7 431m
9. 18 700m
10. 11 040m
11. 9 707m
12. 6 001m

16. 4km
18. 7km

19. Parent/Teacher
20. Parent/Teacher
21. Parent/Teacher
22. Parent/Teacher
23. Parent/Teacher
24. 16 370m
25. 9.242km
26. 431
27. 566
28. 1 181
29. 1 762
30. 719
31.
32.
33.

UNIT 24

1.

2. 127 / 392 / +206 / 725
3. 581 / 35 / + 212 / 828
4. 257 / 76 / + 666 / 999
5. 417 / 188 / +262 / 867
6. 882 / 62 / + 123 / 1067
7. 542 / 30 / + 249 / 821
8. £458
9. £42
10.

11. 1 hectare
12. 5 hectares
13. $\frac{1}{2}$ hectare
14. 8 hectares
15. 100 ha
16. 500 ha
17. 1 000ha
18. 50ha
19. 25ha
20. Parent/Teacher
21. 200 000m^2
22. 20ha
23. $\frac{1}{5}$
24. 5ha

1. 215
2. 337
3. 349
4. 132
5. 169
6. 29
7. (a) 434
   (b) 450
   (c) 268
   (d) 943 - 564 = 379
8. 266 metres
9. 218 metres
10. 48 metres
11. = 451 - 178 = 273
12. = 76 + 39 = 115

13. 9500 metres
14. $1\frac{1}{2}$ ha
15. 800ha
16. 90 000m^2
17. 218 / 160 / + 84 / 462
18. 307 / 244 / + 125 / 676
19. 174 / 382 / + 250 / 806
20. 421 / 346 / +102 / 869
21. 332 / 232 / + 333 / 897
22. 546 / 32 / + 275 / 853
23. 496 / 312 / 184
24. 508 / 427 / 81
25. 759 / 638 / 121
26. 700ha
27. 75ha
28. 25ha
29. 560ha
30. Still at water level

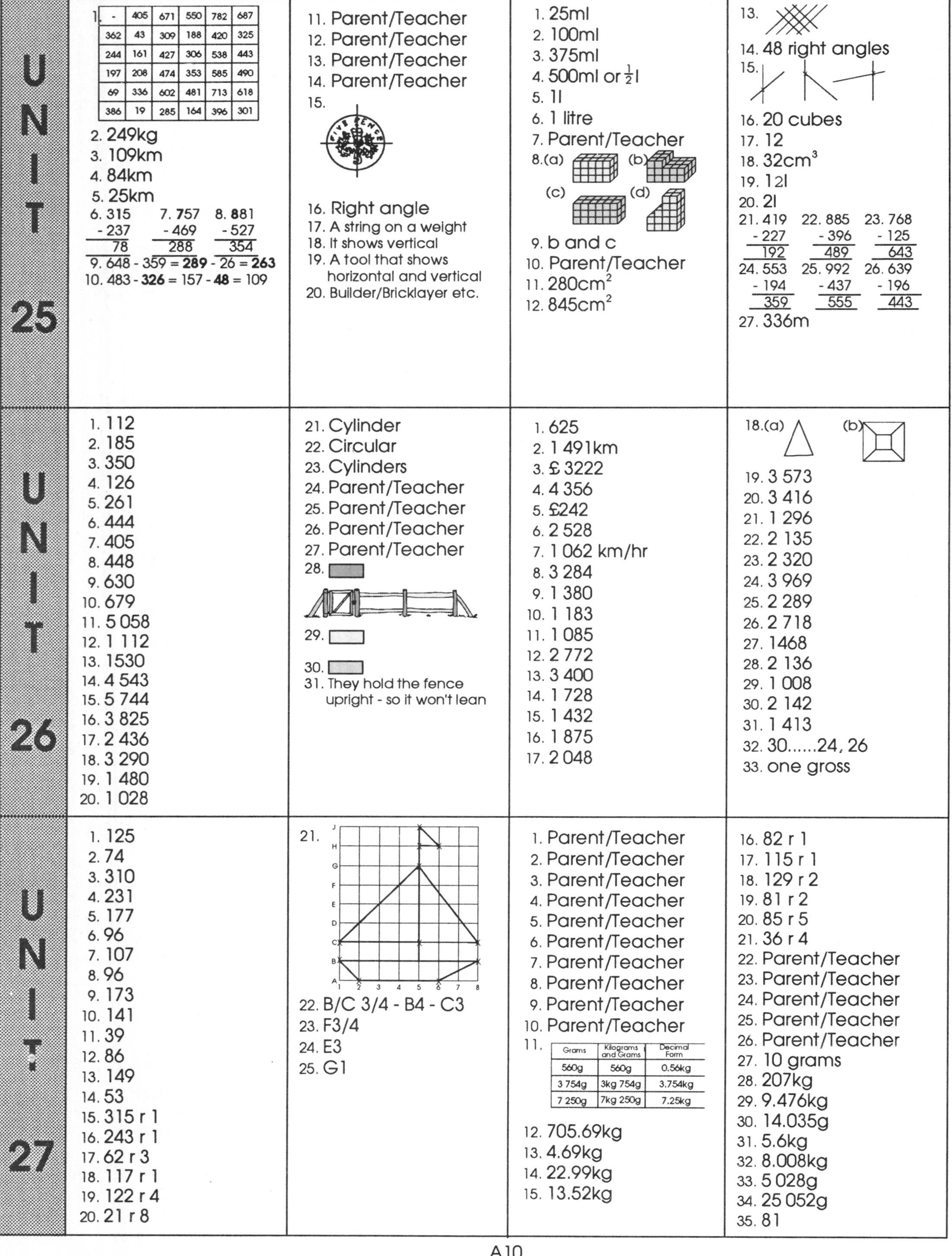

UNIT 25

1.

-	405	671	550	782	687
362	43	309	188	420	325
244	161	427	306	538	443
197	208	474	353	585	490
69	336	602	481	713	618
386	19	285	164	396	301

2. 249kg
3. 109km
4. 84km
5. 25km
6. 315 - 237 = 78
7. **7**57 - 469 = 288
8. **8**81 - 527 = 354
9. 648 - 359 = **289** - 26 = **263**
10. 483 - **326** = 157 - **48** = 109
11. Parent/Teacher
12. Parent/Teacher
13. Parent/Teacher
14. Parent/Teacher
15. (drawing)
16. Right angle
17. A string on a weight
18. It shows vertical
19. A tool that shows horizontal and vertical
20. Builder/Bricklayer etc.

1. 25ml
2. 100ml
3. 375ml
4. 500ml or $\frac{1}{2}$l
5. 1l
6. 1 litre
7. Parent/Teacher
8. (a) (b) (c) (d) (drawings)
9. b and c
10. Parent/Teacher
11. $280cm^2$
12. $845cm^2$

13. (drawing)
14. 48 right angles
15. (drawings)
16. 20 cubes
17. 12
18. $32cm^3$
19. 12l
20. 2l
21. 419 - 227 = 192
22. 885 - 396 = 489
23. 768 - 125 = 643
24. 553 - 194 = 359
25. 992 - 437 = 555
26. 639 - 196 = 443
27. 336m

UNIT 26

1. 112
2. 185
3. 350
4. 126
5. 261
6. 444
7. 405
8. 448
9. 630
10. 679
11. 5 058
12. 1 112
13. 1530
14. 4 543
15. 5 744
16. 3 825
17. 2 436
18. 3 290
19. 1 480
20. 1 028
21. Cylinder
22. Circular
23. Cylinders
24. Parent/Teacher
25. Parent/Teacher
26. Parent/Teacher
27. Parent/Teacher
28. (drawing)
29. (drawing)
30. (drawing)
31. They hold the fence upright - so it won't lean

1. 625
2. 1 491km
3. £ 3222
4. 4 356
5. £242
6. 2 528
7. 1 062 km/hr
8. 3 284
9. 1 380
10. 1 183
11. 1 085
12. 2 772
13. 3 400
14. 1 728
15. 1 432
16. 1 875
17. 2 048

18. (a) (b) (drawings)
19. 3 573
20. 3 416
21. 1 296
22. 2 135
23. 2 320
24. 3 969
25. 2 289
26. 2 718
27. 1468
28. 2 136
29. 1 008
30. 2 142
31. 1 413
32. 30......24, 26
33. one gross

UNIT 27

1. 125
2. 74
3. 310
4. 231
5. 177
6. 96
7. 107
8. 96
9. 173
10. 141
11. 39
12. 86
13. 149
14. 53
15. 315 r 1
16. 243 r 1
17. 62 r 3
18. 117 r 1
19. 122 r 4
20. 21 r 8
21. (grid drawing)
22. B/C 3/4 - B4 - C3
23. F3/4
24. E3
25. G1

1. Parent/Teacher
2. Parent/Teacher
3. Parent/Teacher
4. Parent/Teacher
5. Parent/Teacher
6. Parent/Teacher
7. Parent/Teacher
8. Parent/Teacher
9. Parent/Teacher
10. Parent/Teacher
11.

Grams	Kilograms and Grams	Decimal Form
560g	560g	0.56kg
3 754g	3kg 754g	3.754kg
7 250g	7kg 250g	7.25kg

12. 705.69kg
13. 4.69kg
14. 22.99kg
15. 13.52kg

16. 82 r 1
17. 115 r 1
18. 129 r 2
19. 81 r 2
20. 85 r 5
21. 36 r 4
22. Parent/Teacher
23. Parent/Teacher
24. Parent/Teacher
25. Parent/Teacher
26. Parent/Teacher
27. 10 grams
28. 207kg
29. 9.476kg
30. 14.035g
31. 5.6kg
32. 8.008kg
33. 5 028g
34. 25 052g
35. 81

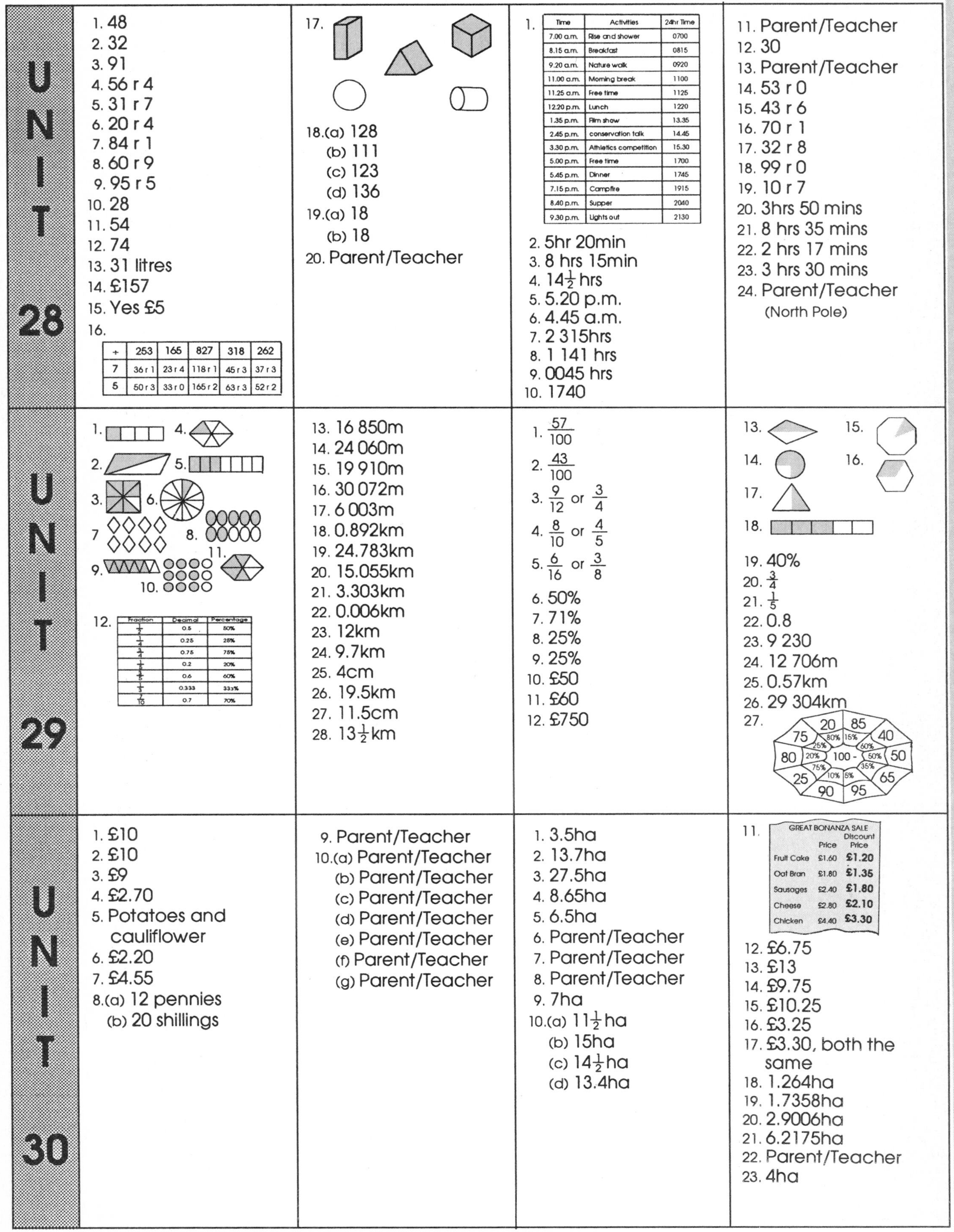

UNIT 28

1. 48
2. 32
3. 91
4. 56 r 4
5. 31 r 7
6. 20 r 4
7. 84 r 1
8. 60 r 9
9. 95 r 5
10. 28
11. 54
12. 74
13. 31 litres
14. £157
15. Yes £5
16.

÷	253	165	827	318	262
7	36 r 1	23 r 4	118 r 1	45 r 3	37 r 3
5	50 r 3	33 r 0	165 r 2	63 r 3	52 r 2

17.

18.(a) 128
(b) 111
(c) 123
(d) 136

19.(a) 18
(b) 18

20. Parent/Teacher

1.

Time	Activities	24hr Time
7.00 a.m.	Rise and shower	0700
8.15 a.m.	Breakfast	0815
9.20 a.m.	Nature walk	0920
11.00 a.m.	Morning break	1100
11.25 a.m.	Free time	1125
12.20 p.m.	Lunch	1220
1.35 p.m.	Film show	13.35
2.45 p.m.	conservation talk	14.45
3.30 p.m.	Athletics competition	15.30
5.00 p.m.	Free time	1700
5.45 p.m.	Dinner	1745
7.15 p.m.	Campfire	1915
8.40 p.m.	Supper	2040
9.30 p.m.	Lights out	2130

2. 5hr 20min
3. 8 hrs 15min
4. $14\frac{1}{2}$ hrs
5. 5.20 p.m.
6. 4.45 a.m.
7. 2 315hrs
8. 1 141 hrs
9. 0045 hrs
10. 1740
11. Parent/Teacher
12. 30
13. Parent/Teacher
14. 53 r 0
15. 43 r 6
16. 70 r 1
17. 32 r 8
18. 99 r 0
19. 10 r 7
20. 3hrs 50 mins
21. 8 hrs 35 mins
22. 2 hrs 17 mins
23. 3 hrs 30 mins
24. Parent/Teacher (North Pole)

UNIT 29

1. 4. 2. 5. 3. 6. 7 8. 9. 10. 11.

12.

Fraction	Decimal	Percentage
$\frac{1}{2}$	0.5	50%
$\frac{1}{4}$	0.25	25%
$\frac{3}{4}$	0.75	75%
$\frac{1}{5}$	0.2	20%
$\frac{3}{5}$	0.6	60%
$\frac{1}{3}$	0.333	33⅓%
$\frac{7}{10}$	0.7	70%

13. 16 850m
14. 24 060m
15. 19 910m
16. 30 072m
17. 6 003m
18. 0.892km
19. 24.783km
20. 15.055km
21. 3.303km
22. 0.006km
23. 12km
24. 9.7km
25. 4cm
26. 19.5km
27. 11.5cm
28. $13\frac{1}{2}$km

1. $\frac{57}{100}$
2. $\frac{43}{100}$
3. $\frac{9}{12}$ or $\frac{3}{4}$
4. $\frac{8}{10}$ or $\frac{4}{5}$
5. $\frac{6}{16}$ or $\frac{3}{8}$
6. 50%
7. 71%
8. 25%
9. 25%
10. £50
11. £60
12. £750

13. 15. 14. 16. 17. 18.

19. 40%
20. $\frac{3}{4}$
21. $\frac{1}{5}$
22. 0.8
23. 9 230
24. 12 706m
25. 0.57km
26. 29 304km
27.

UNIT 30

1. £10
2. £10
3. £9
4. £2.70
5. Potatoes and cauliflower
6. £2.20
7. £4.55
8.(a) 12 pennies
(b) 20 shillings

9. Parent/Teacher
10.(a) Parent/Teacher
(b) Parent/Teacher
(c) Parent/Teacher
(d) Parent/Teacher
(e) Parent/Teacher
(f) Parent/Teacher
(g) Parent/Teacher

1. 3.5ha
2. 13.7ha
3. 27.5ha
4. 8.65ha
5. 6.5ha
6. Parent/Teacher
7. Parent/Teacher
8. Parent/Teacher
9. 7ha
10.(a) $11\frac{1}{2}$ha
(b) 15ha
(c) $14\frac{1}{2}$ha
(d) 13.4ha

11.

GREAT BONANZA SALE

	Price	Discount Price
Fruit Cake	£1.60	**£1.20**
Oat Bran	£1.80	**£1.35**
Sausages	£2.40	**£1.80**
Cheese	£2.80	**£2.10**
Chicken	£4.40	**£3.30**

12. £6.75
13. £13
14. £9.75
15. £10.25
16. £3.25
17. £3.30, both the same
18. 1.264ha
19. 1.7358ha
20. 2.9006ha
21. 6.2175ha
22. Parent/Teacher
23. 4ha

UNIT 31

1. 6 693
2. 14 191
3. 16 059
4. 22 518
5. 7 602
6. 8 081

7. 4931 / 7065 / +2762 / 14758
8. 9131 / 8017 / +3356 / 20504
9. 8276 / 1267 / +4409 / 13952

10. 14758 / 20504 / +13952 / 49214

11. £17 497.04
12. £11 794.27
13. £6 356.21
14. £9 342.70

15. Parent/Teacher

1. £86 122
2. £42 860
3. £16 830
4. £5 385
5. £18 624
6. £600

7. 8 611
8. 7 321
9. 13 651
10. 20 996
11. 14 883
12. 10 448
13. Parent/Teacher

14. 30**7**3 / 7286 / +**5**081 / 15440
15. **9**340 / 762 / +8218 / 18**3**20
16. 10**4**0 / 7063 / +**9**102 / 1720**5**

17. £8 698.94
18. £22 412.72

UNIT 32

1. 355
2. 431
3. 181
4. 434
5. 797
6. 487

7. 294 / - 15 / 279
8. 608 / - 44 / 564
9. 503 / - 18 / 485
10. 711 / - 09 / 702
11. 470 / - 61 / 409
12. 542 / - 63 / 479

13. 286
14. £736
15. 605km
16. 306
17. 207
18. 166

19. Parent/Teacher - the further away something is the smaller it seems.
20. Parent/Teacher
21. Parent/Teacher
22. Parent/Teacher - The pylons further away look smaller because of the perspective.

1. cm^3
2. cm^3
3. m^3
4. m^3
5. m^3
6. m^3
7. cm^3
8. Parent/Teacher
9. Parent/Teacher
10. Parent/Teacher
11. Parent/Teacher
12. Parent/Teacher
13. Parent/Teacher
14. Total weight
15. Weigh the glass full. Weigh the glass empty. Subtract the empty from full glass to find the water's weight.

16. 366
17. 539
18. 686
19. 809
20. 579
21. 446

22. 318 / - 67 / 251
23. 472 / - 53 / 419
24. 883 / - 47 / 836

25. Parent/Teacher
26. Parent/Teacher
27. Parent/Teacher
28. Parent/Teacher
29. Parent/Teacher
30. Parent/Teacher

31. 841 / - 624 / 217
32. 645 / - 487 / 158
33. 569 / - 324 / 245

UNIT 33

1. 208
2. 119
3. 268
4. 144
5. 431
6. 228
7. 806-
   488, 752, 670, 287, 558, 619, 727, 94, 547, 349
   318, 54, 136, 519, 248, 187, 79, 712, 259, 457
8. 319
9. 83
10. 776, 247, 575
11. 823
12. 336

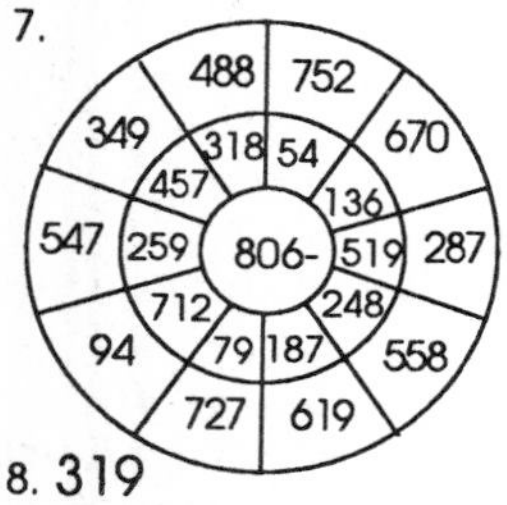

13. Hobb St North and Hope St
14. Judd St and Mitchell St
15. The Mall
16. (a) G4
    (b) J6
    (c) A8
    (d) C10
17. Argyle Place
18. A9 and J11
19. It is too easily confused with number 1.

1. Parent/Teacher
2. Parent/Teacher
3. Parent/Teacher
4.

Days of the week	Min	Max	Difference
Sunday	7°C	15°C	8°C
Monday	9°C	23°C	14°C
Tuesday	9°C	21°C	12°C
Wednesday	10°C	23°C	13°C
Thursday	4°C	27°C	23°C
Friday	6°C	31°C	25°C
Saturday	10°C	33°C	23°C

5. 8°C, 11°C, 19°C, 27°C, 39°C, 68°C
6. 17°C, 25°C, 34°C, 48°C, 51°C, 72°C
7. (a) 98°C (b) 37°C (c) 18°C (d) 74°C
8. -273.15°C

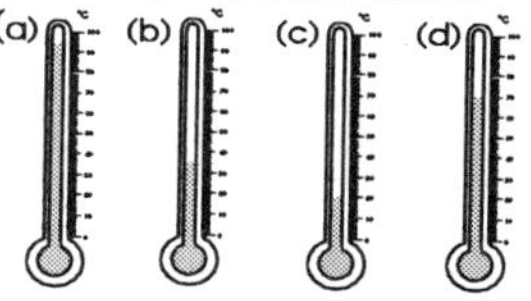

9. 424
10. 309
11. 133
12. 226
13. 269
14. 193
15. 88
16. 99
17. 755
18. 107
19. 141
20. 316
21. 216
22. 8°C, 14°C, 33°C, 39°C, 46°C, 50°C
23. 72°C, 47°C, 31°C, 29°C, 18°C, 16°C

UNIT 34

1. 2 784
2. 2 637
3. 2 115
4. 2 268
5. 1 816
6. 5 292
7. 8 364
8. 10 905
9. 17 528
10. 2072, 4004, 4571, 3283, 296, 572, 653, 469, 2387, 341, 7x, 805, 5635
11. 7 000
12. 9 492kg
13. 19 000
14. 9912, 22248, 12054, 8670, 1652, 3708, 2009, 1445, 14088, 2348, 6 x, 3076, 18456

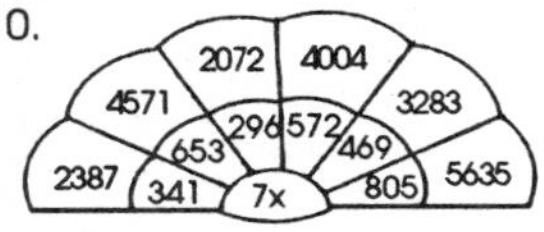

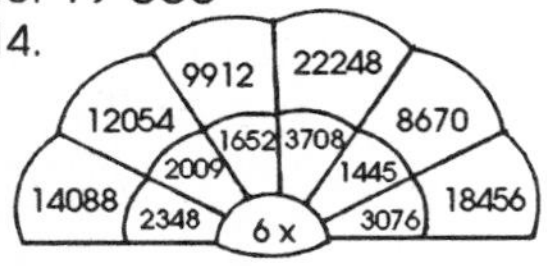

15. (a) 2 mins 25 seconds
    (b) 1 min 17 seconds
    (c) 6 mins 42 sec
    (d) 0 mins 24 sec
    (e) 9 mins 49 sec
    (f) 2 mins 3 sec
16. Parent/Teacher
17. People perform tasks at different speeds.
18. 3 hrs 10 mins 52 secs
19. 14 hrs 25 mins 10 secs
20. 0 hrs 45 mins 35 secs

1. 130 r 2
2. 76 r 5
3. 128 r 3
4. 55 r 3
5. 175 r 1
6. 80 r 4
7. 91 r 3
8. 116 r 1
9. 155 r 2
10. 83 r 2
11. 80 r 0
12. £131
13. £5
14. 97 r 6
15. 2 724
16. 1130 or 4
17. 1 282 r 3
18. 925 r 2
19. 119 r 1
20. 455 r 3

21. 6 544
22. 13 900
23. 18 636
24. 33 796
25. 8 424
26. 22 770
27. Parent/Teacher
28. Parent/Teacher
29. hour hand
30. Only in modern times have more exact measurements become necessary.
31. 140 r 1
32. 133
33. 1 773
34. 883 r 1
35. 828 and one 829
36. 709 r 4

UNIT 35

1. 34
2. £95
3. 47
4. 58km
5. 79
6. 3 left over
7. 130, 3 left over
8. 1438 r 2
9. 474 r 1
10. 945 r 2
11. 958 r 1
12. 345 r 2
13. 821 r 1
14. 40 trips

15. 35
16. 10
17. 50
18. 35
19. 10
20. $720
21. Parent/Teacher
22. Parent/Teacher

1. 0.1, 0.2, 0.3, 0.4, 0.7
2. 0.3, 0.5, 0.6, 0.8, 0.9
3. 0.8, 1.3, 1.7, 1.9, 2.3
4. 1.3, 2.4, 3.4, 4.7, 5.1
5. 1.7, 2.8, 7.1, 7.8, 8.2
6. 3.41
7. 2.7
8. 20.05
9. 4.8
10. 10.01
11. 6.06
12. 1.47m
13. 0.36m
14. 5.09m
15. 9.6m
16. 43.28m
17. £3.45
18. £6.25
19. £5.99
20. £17.55

21. Parent/Teacher
22. 494 r 2
23. 761 r 5
24. 734 r 1
25. 1 548 r 1
26. 39
27. 786 r 3
28. 104 r 3
29. 703 r 3
30. 476p
31. 1108p
32. 2911p
33. 39 87p
34. 10 701p
35. 25 762p
36. 9.01
37. 50.6
38. 100.08
39. 5.03
40. 79.95

UNIT 36

1. 8 916, 19 241, 37 856, 48 375, 58 027, 59 320, 62 717, 83 452
2. Thousand
3. Hundred
4. Ten thousand
5. Unit
6. Two hundred and thirty-seven thousand, three hundred and twenty-five
7. Eight hundred and ninety-one thousand, two hundred and sixty
8. 774
9. 856
10. 18 277
11. £9.15
12. £8.53
13. £575.56
14. 20 980

15. acute 45°
16. right angle 90°
17. acute 60°
18. straight 180°
19. reflex 240°
20. obtuse 120°
21. acute 30°

1. (a) Parent/Teacher
   (b) Parent/Teacher
   (c) Parent/Teacher
   (d) Parent/Teacher
   (e) Parent/Teacher
   (f) Parent/Teacher
   (g) Parent/Teacher
   (h) Parent/Teacher
2. (b) 31cm 8mm
   (c) 46cm 7mm
   (d) 11cm 1mm
   (e) 79cm 2mm
   (f) 127cm 3mm
3. Parent/Teacher
4. 54mm
5. 170mm

6. 45°, 90°, 165°, 135°, 60°, 165°, 115°
7. 6171
8. 15702
9. 12764

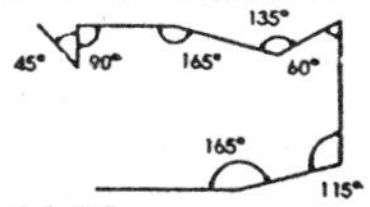

10.	11.	12.
3942	7761	3162
3665	3726	2573
+5714	+2685	+1153
13321	14172	6888

13. (a) 44mm
    (b) 37mm
    (c) 15mm
    (d) 9mm
14. Parent/Teacher
15. Parent/Teacher
16. Parent/Teacher
17. Parent/Teacher
18. 85cm 4mm
19. 13cm 9mm
20. 68cm 2mm

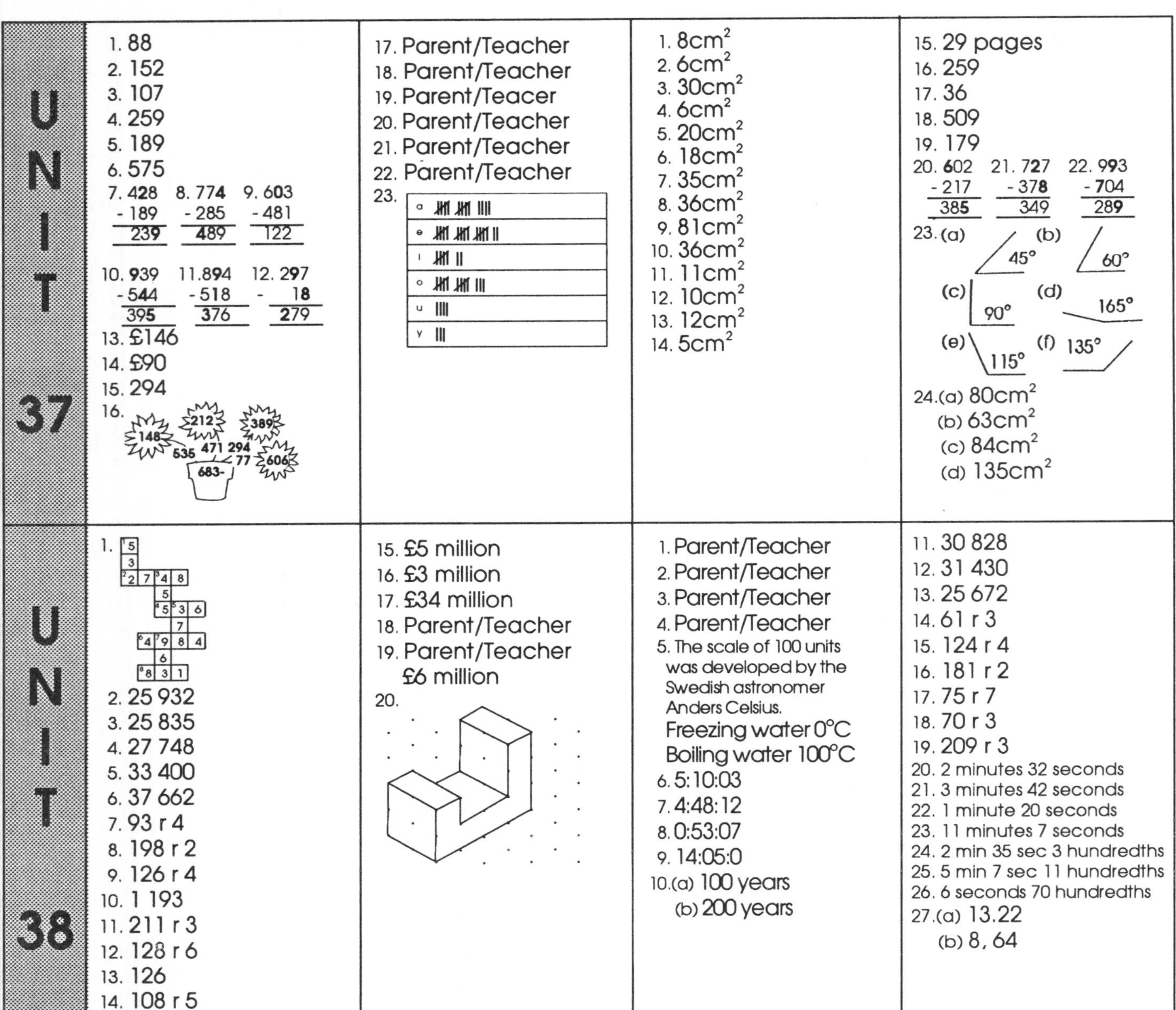

UNIT 37

1. 88
2. 152
3. 107
4. 259
5. 189
6. 575
7. 428 − 189 = 239
8. 774 − 285 = 489
9. 603 − 481 = 122
10. 939 − 544 = 395
11. 894 − 518 = 376
12. 297 − 18 = 279
13. £146
14. £90
15. 294
16.

17. Parent/Teacher
18. Parent/Teacher
19. Parent/Teacer
20. Parent/Teacher
21. Parent/Teacher
22. Parent/Teacher
23.

a	|||| |||| ||||
e	|||| |||| |||| ||
i	|||| ||
o	|||| |||| |||
u	||||
y	|||

1. 8cm^2
2. 6cm^2
3. 30cm^2
4. 6cm^2
5. 20cm^2
6. 18cm^2
7. 35cm^2
8. 36cm^2
9. 81cm^2
10. 36cm^2
11. 11cm^2
12. 10cm^2
13. 12cm^2
14. 5cm^2

15. 29 pages
16. 259
17. 36
18. 509
19. 179
20. 602 − 217 = 385
21. 727 − 378 = 349
22. 993 − 704 = 289
23. (a) 45° (b) 60° (c) 90° (d) 165° (e) 115° (f) 135°
24. (a) 80cm^2
    (b) 63cm^2
    (c) 84cm^2
    (d) 135cm^2

UNIT 38

1.

2. 25 932
3. 25 835
4. 27 748
5. 33 400
6. 37 662
7. 93 r 4
8. 198 r 2
9. 126 r 4
10. 1 193
11. 211 r 3
12. 128 r 6
13. 126
14. 108 r 5
15. £5 million
16. £3 million
17. £34 million
18. Parent/Teacher
19. Parent/Teacher
    £6 million
20.

1. Parent/Teacher
2. Parent/Teacher
3. Parent/Teacher
4. Parent/Teacher
5. The scale of 100 units was developed by the Swedish astronomer Anders Celsius.
   Freezing water 0°C
   Boiling water 100°C
6. 5:10:03
7. 4:48:12
8. 0:53:07
9. 14:05:0
10. (a) 100 years
    (b) 200 years

11. 30 828
12. 31 430
13. 25 672
14. 61 r 3
15. 124 r 4
16. 181 r 2
17. 75 r 7
18. 70 r 3
19. 209 r 3
20. 2 minutes 32 seconds
21. 3 minutes 42 seconds
22. 1 minute 20 seconds
23. 11 minutes 7 seconds
24. 2 min 35 sec 3 hundredths
25. 5 min 7 sec 11 hundredths
26. 6 seconds 70 hundredths
27. (a) 13.22
    (b) 8, 64

Notes

Notes

Notes

Write the **fractions** in **decimal** form and then as **percentages** to finish the table.

Fraction	Decimal	Percentage
1. $\frac{1}{2}$		
2. $\frac{1}{4}$		
3. $\frac{3}{4}$		
4. $\frac{4}{10}$		
5. $\frac{7}{10}$		
6. $\frac{9}{10}$		
7. $\frac{5}{20}$		
8. $\frac{15}{20}$		
9. $\frac{20}{50}$		
10. $\frac{35}{50}$		

11. A track suit is advertised at £ 80, with a discount of $\frac{1}{4}$. What is the selling price? ______

12. A television set is advertised $\frac{1}{3}$ off the price of $600. How much is the television? ______

13. Ladies shoes are £ 50 less 20%. What is the new price? ______

14. A fishing rod, usually £ 160, is reduced by 25%. How much is the rod with the discount? ______

15. *BRAIN STRETCHER:* At a 25% off everything sale a jacket sells for £ 75. What was the original price? ______

16. At the same sale a pair of roller blades were £ 60. What was the original price? ______

17. Write the two **temperatures** and the **difference** between them.

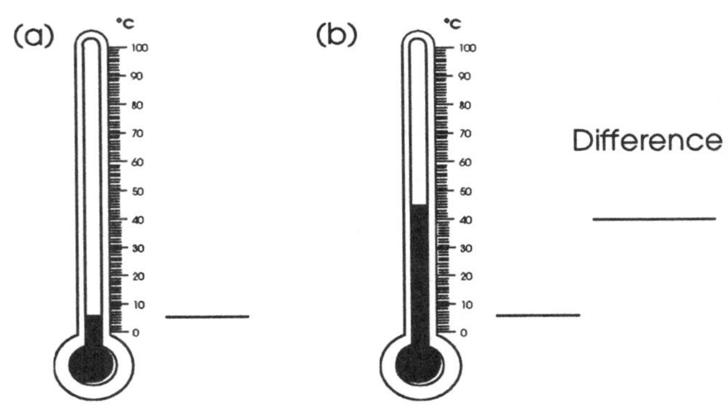

Difference ______

18. Record the **temperatures** and the **difference** between these thermometers.

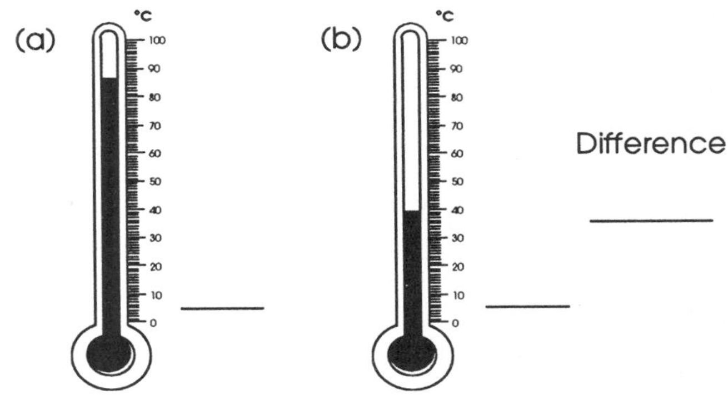

Difference ______

19. The minimum temperature on a summer day is 5°C and the maximum is 26°C. What is the difference in temperature for that day? ______

Express these **fractions** as **percentages.**

20. $\frac{6}{10}$ ______
21. $\frac{10}{20}$ ______
22. $\frac{30}{50}$ ______
23. $\frac{8}{10}$ ______
24. $\frac{4}{5}$ ______
25. $\frac{24}{50}$ ______
26. $\frac{2}{10}$ ______
27. $\frac{2}{5}$ ______

All these items are discounted 25%. Give the new price beside each one.

28.  £ 120

29. 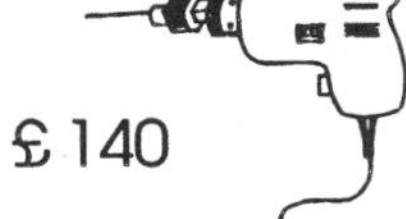 £ 140

30. £ 80 

31. £ 88 

These items are advertised by a jewellery shop.

£ 39.95

£ 54.00

£ 48.00

silver braclet

£ 31.60

£ 99.00

£ 34.53

£ 46.75

£ 95.00

1. How much should one wine glass **cost?** _____

2. If the clock is 50% off original price what was that **price?** _____

3. Any two items over £100 have £10 taken off the **cost.** How much for the jewellery box and man's watch? _____

4. The silver bracelet and gold bangle are bought together. What is the price? _____

5. A 25% **discount** is offered on the gold bangle. How much do I pay? _____

6. The **profit** margin on the jewellery box is £40. How much did it cost the shop? _____

7. A silver bracelet with locket, a clock and set of glasses were bought. The bill showed £ 113.55. What should the **price** be? _____

This **graph** shows food consumed by a family in one week.

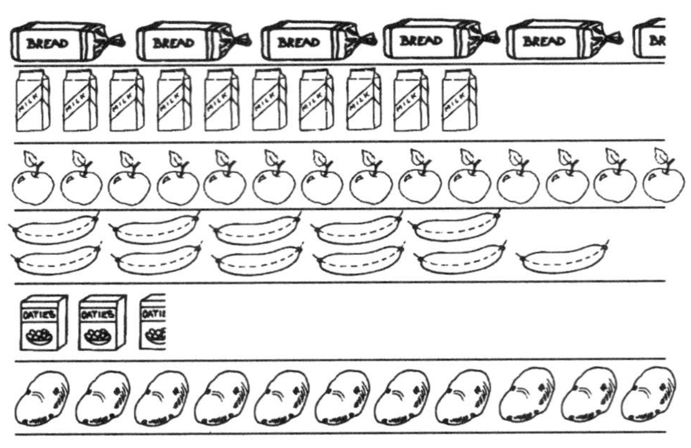

8. How many loaves of bread were eaten? _____

9. How many potatoes? _____

10. How many sausages? _____

11. How many pieces of fruit? _____

12. How many packets of cereal? _____

13. Write four other foods the family may have eaten that are not on the graph.

(a) _____________ (b) _____________

(c) _____________ (d) _____________

14. Estimate how many people there might be in this household. _____

15. In a school orchestra there are **2** pianists, **6** violinists, **4** cellists, **3** percussionists, **1** flautist and **3** trombone players. Make up symbols for each player and draw a picture graph.

Write these **p.m.** times on the **24 hour digital** watches.

1. 7:20 p.m.

2. 11:55 p.m.

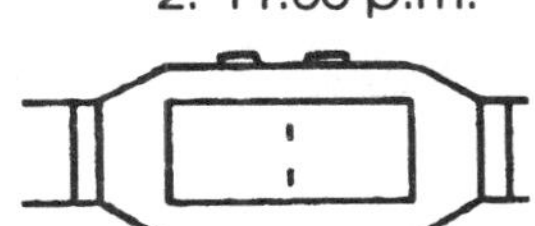

3. 2:36 p.m.

4. 5:24 p.m.

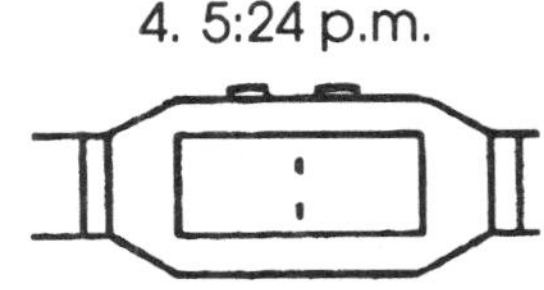

Write these **24 hour times** in **a.m.** or **p.m.** time.

5. 

____

6. 

____

7. 

____

8. 

____

This is a time line of some inventions.

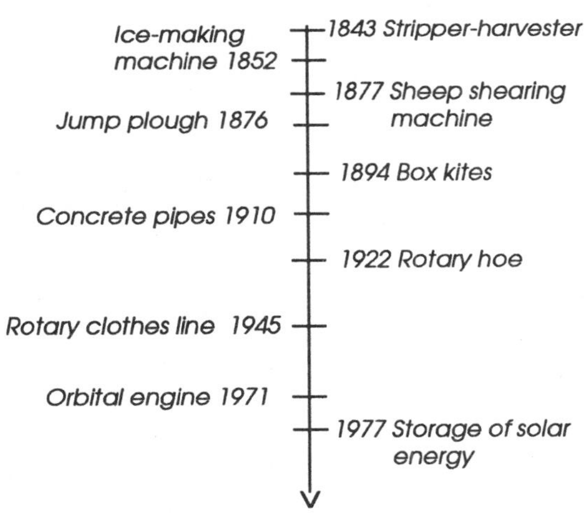

9. How many years between the invention of the stripper-harvester and the sheep shearing machine? _______

10. How many years between the jump plough and orbital engine? _______

11. How many years does this time line cover? _______

12. The Victa lawnmower was invented in 1952. Add this to the time line in the right position. _______

13. A pack of 6 crumpets cost 42p. A pack of 4 cost 32p. Which is the better buy? _______

14. Cooking oil is advertised at £4 per large bottle. It has been reduced 20%. What was its original price? _______

15. An 800g pack of Chocipops cereal sells for £2.40. A 400g pack sells for £1.10. Which is the better buy? _______

16. A gift voucher is offered for every £10 spent at a shop. One customer spends £126.50. How many vouchers are given? _______

17. When it's 11:15 a.m. in Brisbane it's 3:15 a.m. in Athens the same day. What's the time difference? _______

18. A plane is due to take off at 0945 hours and land in Manila at 1720 hours. How long is the flight? _______

Write these times on the analog clocks.

19. 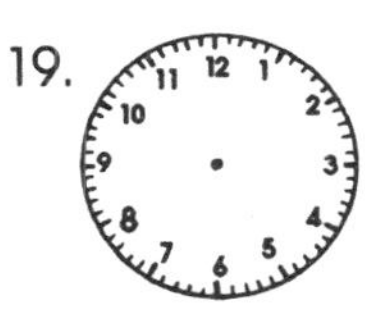
1750 hrs

20. 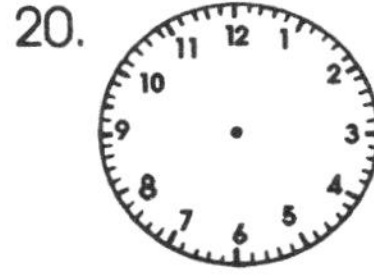
2320 hrs

21 
0110 hrs

Write these p.m. analog times in 24 hour form.

22. 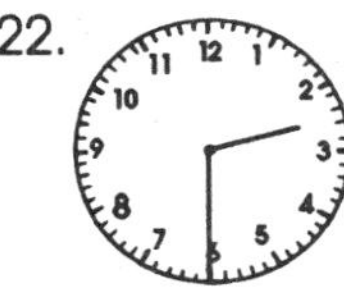
____

23. 
____

24. 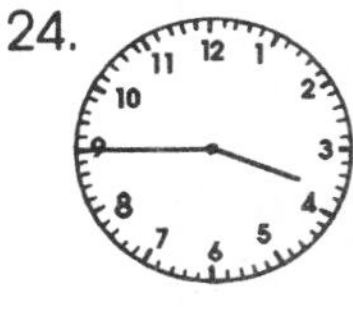
____

Christopher Columbus was born in A.D. 1451 and died in A.D. 1506.

25. For how long did he live? _______

26. How long ago did he die? _______

1. Write these amounts to the nearest pound.

£7 . 43   £26 . 78   £19 . 56   £33 . 27

______ ______ ______ ______

2. Which is the better buy: 1 kg of soap powder at £3 or 2 kg at £5.25?

____

3. Is it better to buy 2l of cooking oil at £2.50 or 6l at £7.95?

____

4. A shop **marks up** its prices 50% on cost. Here are the **cost prices**; give the **selling prices**.

£40   £18   £34   £50   £26

_____ _____ _____ _____ _____

5. At the same shop, these are the **selling prices**. What are the **cost prices**?

£30   £15   £27   £9   £18

_____ _____ _____ _____ _____

6. A TV's marked price is £450. A £20 discount is given in addition to £120 trade-in. If there is a delivery cost of £15, what is the final price of the TV? ______

7. Write a short explanation of these terms:

(a) Invoice: ______________________

____

(b) Discount: ______________________

____

(c) Put aside: ______________________

____

(d) Overheads: ______________________

____

Here is a tally of coins found in a piggy bank

Coin	Tally	Coin	Tally
5 pence	卌 卌 卌 卌 I	10 pence	卌 卌 卌 卌
20 pence	卌 卌 卌 卌 卌 II	50 pence	卌 卌 卌 I
One pound	卌 卌 卌 III	2 pence	卌 卌 I

8. Make a picture graph of the coins. Use small circles only. In some cases you may need to use a second row.

Coin	
5 pence	
10 pence	
20 pence	
50 pence	
One pound	
2 pence	

9. How much in pound coins? ______

10. How much in 20 pence coins? ______

11. How much in 5 pence coins? ______

12. What is the total value of all the silver coins? ______

13. What is the value of the gold coins? ______

14. What is the total value of coins in the graph? ______

15. How much would need to be added to total £60? ______

Write these numbers in words.

1. 26 491 ______________________________

____

2. 48 715 ______________________________

____

3. 79 042 ______________________________

____

4. 6 294 ______________________________

____

Write these words as numbers.

5. Fifty-seven thousand five hundred and twenty-eight __________

6. Sixty-one thousand eight hundred and fifteen __________

7. Eighty thousand three hundred and seven __________

8. Five thousand and four __________

Write the numbers in the correct columns.

	T'Th	Th	H	T	U
9. 62 173					
10. 98 942					
11. 2 015					
12. 39 437					
13. 10 010					
14. 738					
15. 26					
16. 6 859					
17. 25 613					
18. 53 009					

19. A shop **marks up** everything 50% on the **wholesale price**. Fill in the **retail prices**.

Wholesale	Retail
£20	
£44	
£8.60	
£66	

Wholesale	Retail
£30.50	
£18.40	
£2.30	
£23.70	

20. At the same shop, if these were the **retail** prices, what are the **wholesale** prices?

Retail	Wholesale
£60	
£21	
£81	
£36	

Retail	Wholesale
£150	
£180	
£66	
£51.60	

Write these words as numbers.

21. Twenty-seven thousand six hundred and nine __________

22. Forty-eight thousand two hundred and seventy-one __________

23. Eighty-one thousand five hundred and seventeen __________

Write the **value** of numbers in bold.

24. 6**3** 497 ____________________

25. **8**3 054 ____________________

26. 61 37**2** ____________________

27. **8** 074 ____________________

28. Add 2 567 to these numbers.

(a) 18 777 __________ (b) 6 678 __________

Write these numbers in **expanded form**.

1. 28 714________+______+______+______+____

2. 56 425________+______+______+______+____

3. 98 043________+______+______+______+____

4. 6 497 ________+______+______+______+____

5. 90 909________+______+______+______+____

Write the next number.

6. 41 609 ________ 7. 85 650 ________

8. 20 219 ________ 9. 38 900 ________

10. 4 706 ________ 11. 999 ________

12. Complete the **addition** web.

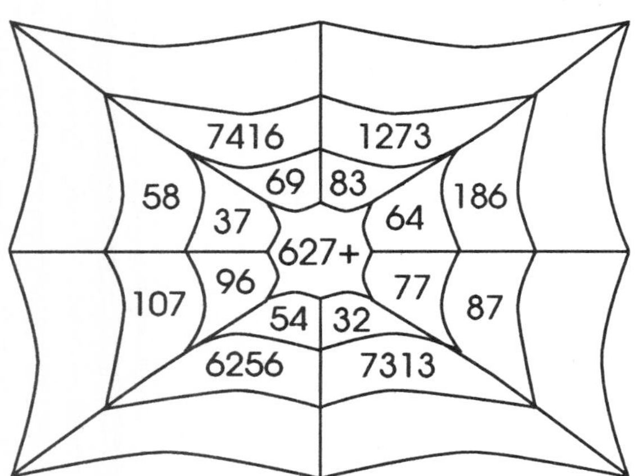

Write the number that comes two before each of these.

13. 56 701 ________ 14. 2 781 ________

15. 3 102 ________ 16. 6 000 ________

17. 95 711 ________ 18. 17 947 ________

Write the **value** for the numbers in bold.

19. 16 **2**73 ________ 20. **8**2 154 ________

Name these **3-D** shapes.

21.  22.  23. 

____________ ____________ ____________

24. Find, draw and name three **cone** shaped objects used at home or at school.

(a) (b) (c)

____________ ____________ ____________

25. Draw and name three **cylinder** shaped objects you might find at home or at school.

(a) (b) (c)

____________ ____________ ____________

26. Think of home or school, and draw and name three **spheres** you might find there.

(a) (b) (c)

____________ ____________ ____________

27. Draw a cylinder shaped object you might find in a park.

This is a **timetable** for buses running between the City and Blue Hills.

	am	am	am	pm	pm	pm	pm	pm
City	8:00	8:20	10:05	2:00	4:40	5:05	5:20	5:50
City North	8:07	8:27	10:12	2:07	4:47	5:15	5:27	5:57
Albert St	8:36	8:56	10:41	2:36	5:21	5:46	6:01	6:31
Jason St	8:40	9:00	10:45	2:40	5:25	5:50	6:05	6:35
Green Park	8:43	9:03	10:48	2:43	5:28	5:53	6:08	6:38
Oxford Junctn.	8:45	9:05	10:50	2:45	5:30	5:55	6:10	6:40
The Mall	8:47	9:07	10:52	2:47	5:32	5:57	6:12	6:42
Blue Hills	8:53	9:13	10:58	2:53	5:39	6:04	6:19	6:49

1. What time does the first bus leave Jason St for Blue Hills? ________
2. At what time does the last bus leave Green Park for Blue Hills? ________
3. How long does it take the 4:40 p.m. bus from City to reach Blue Hills? ________
4. If you miss the 10:45 a.m. bus at Jason Street, what time does the next bus leave? ________
5. How long is the journey from City North to Oxford Junction?________
6. If the 5:20 p.m. bus leaves City 15 minutes late, what time would you expect it to reach the Mall? ________
7. If you miss the 4:40 p.m. bus, and catch the next, what time will you reach Green Park? ________
8. How long between the first bus leaving City in the morning and the first bus in the afternoon leaving City? ________
9. If you miss the 5:15 a.m. bus at City North, how long before the next bus? ________
10. How long is the journey from Albert St to Oxford Junction? ________

11. Write four different everyday examples of **rectangular prisms**.

    (a) ________________________

    (b) ________________________

    (c) ________________________

    (d) ________________________

12. Children like to eat a **sphere** on top of a **cone**. What could I be thinking of? ________
13. Where are some of the world's famous **pyramids**?________
14. A tourist coach leaves a town at 1100 hours and arrives at the next town at 1320 hours. How long did the trip take? ________
15. If the bus in question 14 stopped 15 minutes for fuel, how long was the bus on the road? ________

Write the number that comes 12 after each of these.

16. 39 204 ________ 17. 86 757 ________

18. 5 094 ________ 19. 12 112 ________

20. 23 619 ________ 21. 4 711 ________

Write the number that comes 8 before each of these.

22. 27 490 ________ 23. 6 238 ________

24. 79 516 ________ 25. 45 317 ________

26. Draw a **triangular prism**.

1.
```
  192
   27
+ 401
```

2.
```
  316
  425
+ 379
```

3.
```
  483
    7
+  34
```

4.
```
  376
  295
+ 217
```

5.
```
  278
  348
+ 296
```

6.
```
    9
  826
+  93
```

7. 193 + 72 + 9 + 103 = ______

8. 248 + 7 + 123 + 325 = ______

A mail order company advertised these products.

£105
Exercise bike

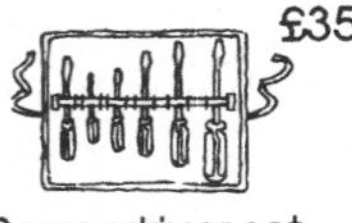
£35
Screwdriver set

Underwater watch
£90

£30
Coffee maker

£190
Starfinder telescope

£80
Computer stand

£140
Three-drawer chest

Car stereo
£100

Fill in the prices on the order forms.

9.
Please send me	£
Computer stand	
Underwater watch	
Three-drawer chest	______
Total	

10.
Please send me	£
Starfinder telescope	
Coffee maker	
Car stereo	______
Total	

11.
Please send me	£
Exercise bike	
Screwdrivers	
Underwater watch	______
Total	

12.
Please send me	£
Computer stand	
Coffee maker	
Exercise bike	______
Total	

13. Fill in the table

3-D shape	Name	Faces	Edges	Corners

14. Draw what you would see when these **3-D** objects are cut as shown.

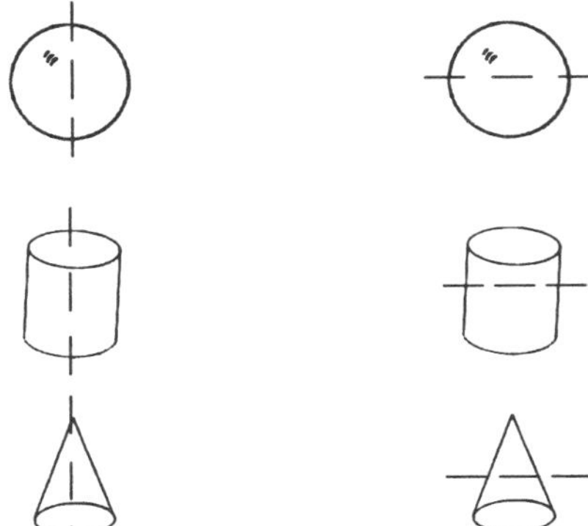

15. In this modern painting, colour the spheres red, cones blue and cylinders green.

16. Draw party decorations or items based on each of these **3-D** objects.

sphere *cone* *cylinder*

Change these **metres** to **kilometres**.

1. 560 m ________
2. 1 325 m________
3. 9 611 m ________
4. 14 707 m________
5. 12 580 m ________
6. 51 163 m________

Change these **kilometres** to **metres**.

7. 2.35 km ________
8. 7.431 km________
9. 18. 7 km ________
10. 11.04 km ________
11. 9.707 km ________
12. 6.001 km ________

Complete the map using a scale of 1 cm = 1 km.

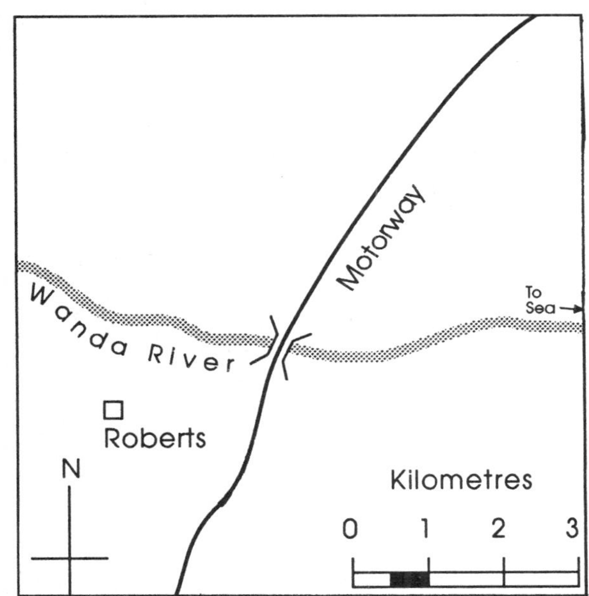

13. Add the town of Boyd, on the western side of the motorway, 3 km north of the bridge.
14. Add the town of Nolan, 3 km upriver from the bridge.
15. Draw a road joining Boyd and Nolan.
16. How long is the Boyd to Nolan road? ________
17. Draw a road from Roberts, due east to the motorway.
18. How long is the river shown on the map? ________
19. Draw part of a main road, $7\frac{1}{2}$ km long (Scale 1 cm = 1 km).
20. Two kilometres along the road from the western end is a bridge. Show it on the road above.
21. $1\frac{1}{2}$ km further on from the bridge is a service station. Mark it S on the road.
22. $1\frac{1}{2}$ km from the eastern end of the road is a rail crossing. Show this.
23. 5km from the western end, a minor road joins the main road from the north. Show this.
24. How many **metres** in 16.37 km?
25. How many **kilometres** in 9 242 m?________
26. 116 + 290 + 17 + 8 = ________
27. 290 + 83 + 154 + 39 = ________
28. 605 + 324 + 69 + 183 = ________
29. 486 + 721 + 463 + 92 = ________
30. 261 + 212 + 237 + 9 = ________

Draw what you see when these **3-D** shapes are cut as shown.

31. 32.  33. 

Unit 24

1. Fill in the **addition** web.

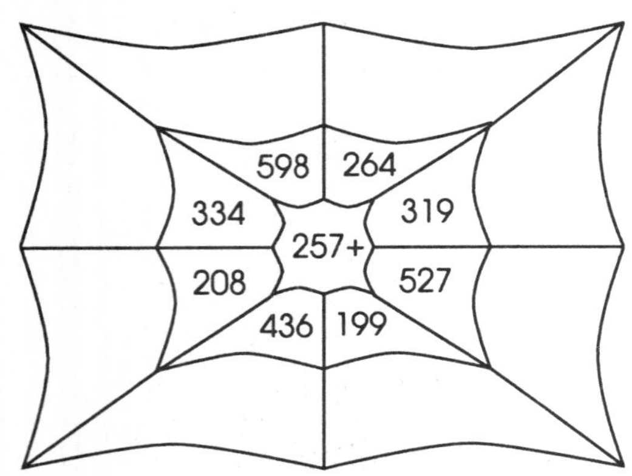

Fill in the spaces.

2\.
```
  1 2 7
  3 9 _
+ _ 0 6
-------
  7 2 5
```

3\.
```
  _ 8 1
    3 _
+ 2 1 2
-------
  8 2 8
```

4\.
```
  2 5 _
    7 6
+ 6 _ 6
-------
  9 9 9
```

5\.
```
  4 1 7
  1 _ 8
+ 2 6 _
-------
  8 6 7
```

6\.
```
  8 _ 2
    6 _
+ _ 2 3
-------
 1 0 6 7
```

7\.
```
  _ 4 2
    3 _
+ 2 4 9
-------
  8 _ 1
```

8. A lady bought items of furniture worth £78, £209 and £154. She was charged £17 for delivery. How much did she pay? ________

9. If she gave $500 to pay for the furniture, what change would she receive? ________

10. Complete the jumbo addition number wheel.

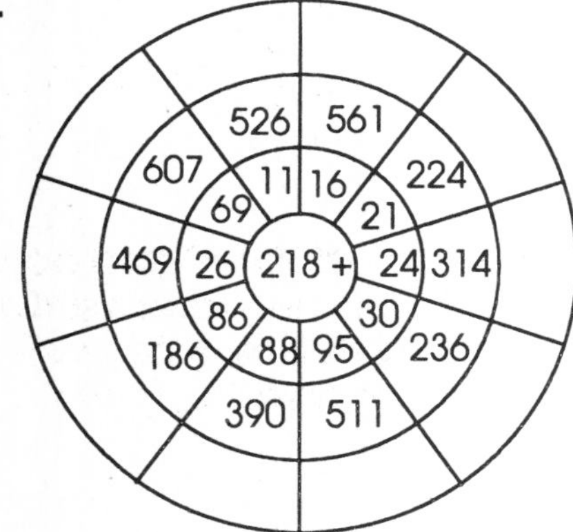

Write these **areas** as **hectares**.

11. 10 000 square metres ________

12. 50 000 square metres ________

13. 5 000 square metres ________

14. 80 000 square metres ________

15. How many **hectares** in one **square kilometre**? ________

16. 5 square kilometres = ______ hectares

17. 10 square kilometres = ______ hectares

18. $\frac{1}{2}$ square kilometre = ______ hectares

19. $\frac{1}{4}$ square kilometre = ______ hectares

20. Using a **scale** of 1cm = 100m draw an **area** 500m x 400m. Write the measurements on the inside.

21. How many **square metres** in the **area** above? ________

22. How many **hectares**? ________

23. What fraction of a **square kilometre** is this area? ________

24. If the area was divided into 4 equal parts, how many hectares in each part? ________

1.
```
  300
-  85
-----
```

2.
```
  500
- 163
-----
```

3.
```
  425
-  76
-----
```

4.
```
  269
- 137
-----
```

5.
```
  378
- 209
-----
```

6.
```
  198
- 169
-----
```

7. An alien from Zoot had 943 rivets. He knew he needed to have 379 left after repairing his saucer. On Zoot he hadn't learnt subtraction.

(a) First he took away 509 and found he had ______

(b) Then he took away 493 and found he had ______

(c) Then he took away 675 and found he had ______

(d) Finally he worked out

______ - ______ = 379

8. Black Mountain is 613m above sea level. Green Mountain is 347m above sea level. What is the difference? ______

9. Mount Mighty is 565 m high. How much higher is this than Green Mountain? ______

10. How far would you climb down from the top of Black Mountain to the top of Mount Mighty? ______

11. 863 - 412 = ______ - 178 = ______

12. 254 - 178 = ______ + 39 = ______

13. A distance on a map is $9\frac{1}{2}$ cm, and the scale is 1 cm = 1 km. How far is this in metres? ______

14. How many **hectares** in 15 000 m²? ______

15. How many **hectares** in 8km²? ______

16. Six blocks of land have an area of $1\frac{1}{2}$ hectares each. How many square metres altogether? ______

Fill in the missings numbers.

17.
```
  2 1 8
  1 6 0
+   8 _
-------
  4 6 2
```

18.
```
  3 _ 7
  2 4 4
+ 1 2 5
-------
  _ 7 6
```

19.
```
  1 7 _
  3 8 2
+ _ 5 0
-------
  8 0 6
```

20.
```
  4 _ 1
  3 4 6
+ _ 0 2
-------
  8 6 _
```

21.
```
  _ 3 2
  2 _ 2
+ 3 3 _
-------
  8 9 7
```

22.
```
  _ 4 6
    3 _
+ 2 7 5
-------
  8 _ 3
```

23.
```
  _ 9 6
- 3 1 2
-------
  1 8 4
```

24.
```
  5 _ 8
- 4 2 7
-------
    8 _
```

25.
```
  _ 5 9
- 6 _ 8
-------
  1 2 _
```

Write these areas as **hectares**.

26. 7 square kilometres = ______ ha

27. $\frac{3}{4}$ square kilometre = ______ ha

28. 0.25 square kilometre = ______ ha

29. 5.6 square kilometres = ______ ha

30. A ship's rope ladder hanging down the side just touches the water's surface at low tide. The tide rises 3 m; where will the bottom of the ladder be now?

____

Unit 25

1. Fill in the **subtraction** grid. Use a calculator to check answers.

-	405	671	550	782	687
362					
244					
197				585	
69					
386					

2. A greengrocery had 693 kg of potatoes to sell. During a day it sold 444 kg. How many kilograms left? ______

A motorist drove 249 km on Monday, 165 km on Tuesday and 274 km on Wednesday.

3. How many more kilometres on Wednesday than Tuesday? ______

4. How many fewer kilometres on Tuesday than Monday? ______

5. How many more kilometres would need to be driven on Monday to equal Wednesday's total? ______

Fill in the missing numbers in these **algorithms**.

6.
```
  3 _ 5
- 2 3 7
-------
    7 _
```

7.
```
  _ 5 7
- 4 6 9
-------
    2 _
```

8.
```
  _ 8 1
- 5 _ 7
-------
  3 5 _
```

9. 648 - 359 = ______ - 26 = ______

10 . 483 - ______ = 157 - ______ = 109

11. Draw three **horizontal** lines.

12. Draw three **vertical** lines.

13. Draw 4 **horizontal** lines and 4 **vertical** lines, so they cross and make a pattern.

14. Where might you see the pattern above in the environment?

______

______

15. Show the horizontal and vertical axes (lines) on this 5 pence coin.

16. What is the angle formed between the two axes? ______

17. What is a **plumb line**? ______

______

18. What does a **plumb line** show?

______

19. What is a **spirit level**? ______

______

20. Who might use a spirit level? ______

Write the equivalent **volumes** in **millilitres**. Use the short form. The first one is done for you.

1. 25 cubic centimetres = 25ml
2. 100 cubic centimetres = ______
3. 375 cubic centimetres = ______
4. 500 cubic centimetres = ______
5. 1 000 cubic centimetres = ______
6. Express 1 000 ml in litres = ______
7. Build these four models, using blocks.

(a) 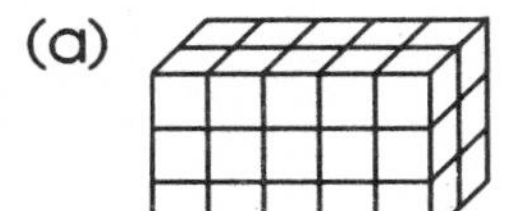 

(b) 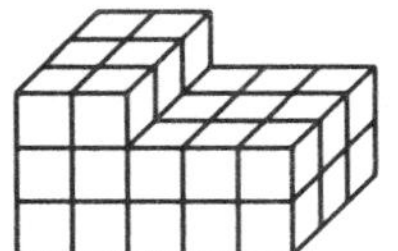

(c) 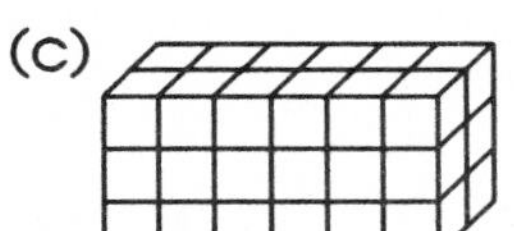

(d) 

8. Use colour to indicate if any of the objects in question 7 have the same **volume**.
9. Which prism(s) in (7) have the greatest volume(s)? ______
10. Take 24 cubes and make three different 8-cube prisms. Draw them here.

11. Write 280 ml in cm^3. ______
12. Write 845 ml in cm^3. ______

13. Draw three lines that cross these four at **right angles**.

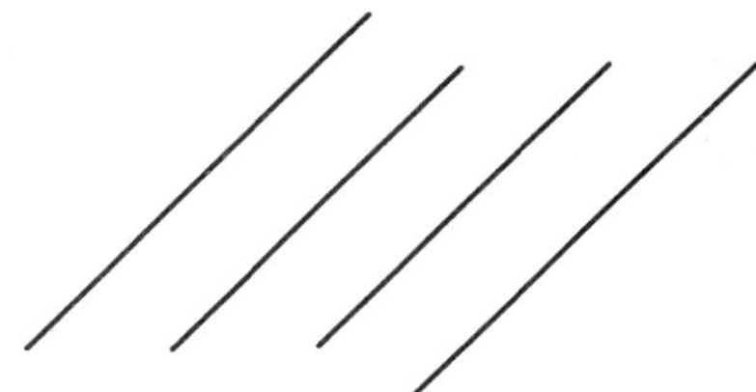

14. How many right angles are there in the diagram above? ______

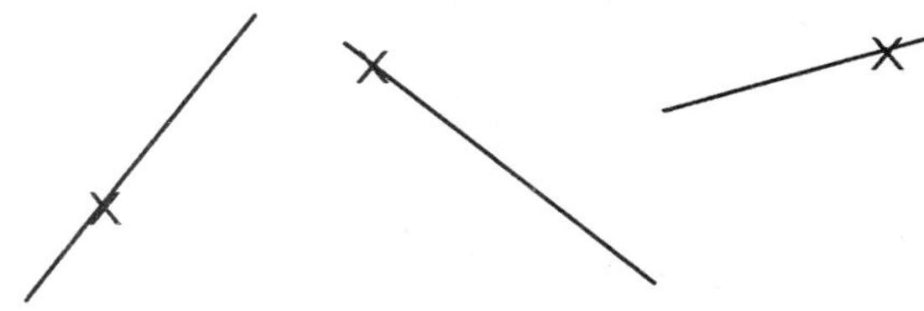

15. Draw vertical lines at the points marked x on these lines.

16. How many cubes in this object? ______
17. How many cubes are needed to turn it into a rectangular prism? ______
18. If each cube is a cubic centimetre, what would the total volume of the prism be? ______

19. 1 500 cm^3 = ______ l 20. 2 000 cm^3 = ______ l

21.
```
  _ 1 9
- 2 2 _
-------
  1 9 2
```

22.
```
  8 _ 5
- 3 9 6
-------
  _ 8 _
```

23.
```
  _ 6 _
- 1 _ 5
-------
  6 4 3
```

24.
```
  _ 5 3
- 1 _ 4
-------
  3 5 _
```

25.
```
  9 _ 2
- _ 3 _
-------
  5 5 5
```

26.
```
  6 3 _
- 1 _ 6
-------
  4 4 3
```

27. A parachutist jumps out of a plane at 950 m and opens her 'chute at 614 m. How far did she free fall? ______

1. 28 x 4 = ____
2. 37 x 5 = ____
3. 50 x 7 = ____
4. 63 x 2 = ____
5. 87 x 3 = ____
6. 74 x 6 = ____
7. 45 x 9 = ____
8. 56 x 8 = ____
9. 70 x 9 = ____
10. 97 x 7 = ____
11. 562 x 9 = ____
12. 278 x 4 = ____
13. 306 x 5 = ____
14. 649 x 7 = ____
15. 718 x 8 = ____

16. At the tennis club **425** seats are in each row of section A. If there are **9** rows, how many seats are there in section A? ____

17. Terry had **348** stamps in each of his **7** albums. How many stamps altogether? ____

18. There were **658** visitors each day to the museum. How many visitors in **5** days? ____

19. One hundred and eighty-five Scouts are in each group at a jamboree. If there are **8** groups, how many Scouts altogether? ____

20. There are **257** jellybeans in a jar. How many jellybeans in **4** jars? ____

21. What **3-D** object is the birthday cake? ____

22. What **2-D** shape is the plate beneath the cake? ____

23. What **3-D** objects are the candles? ____

24. Draw a **wavy** pattern of icing around the top of the cake.

25. Draw a pattern of **intersecting lines** around the plate.

26. Light the candles by drawing tiny **ovals** for the flames.

27. Draw dotted lines to show where the first slice of cake will be cut. *(The cake is divided into 8 pieces.)*

28. Colour all the **vertical** posts in the fence and gate red.

29. Colour all the **horizontal** timber green.

30. Colour the sloping posts brown.

31. Why are there **diagonal** pieces of timber on each end?

____

____

____

1. A train carriage holds **125** people seated. If there are **5** carriages, how many people on the train? _______

2. One lap of a race track is **7km** long. A racing car covers **213** laps. How far does it travel? _______

3. Television sets cost **£537** each. Six are bought. How much will they cost altogether? _______

4. Buns for a cake sale are packed in trays of **9.** If all of **484** children sell one tray, how many buns? _______

5. The trays are sold for **50p** each. How much money raised? _______

6. A park has **316** tulips in each of **8** rows. How many tulips? _______

7. The top speed of a car is **118km/h.** A jet can fly nine times faster. How fast is that? _______

8. 821 x 4 = ____	9. 276 x 5 = ____	10. 169 x 7 = ____
11. 217 x 5 = ____	12. 396 x 7 = ____	13. 425 x 8 = ____
14. 432 x 4 = ____	15. 179 x 8 = ____	16. 625 x 3 = ____

17. Germs in a laboratory double in number every hour. If there are **128** germs at 8.00 a.m., how many germs by midday? _______

18. Show the shape of each pyramid you would see when it is cut as shown.

(a)

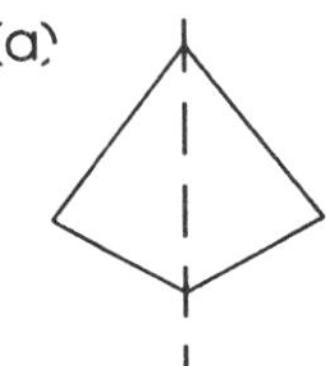

(b)

19. 397 x 9 = ____	20. 427 x 8 = ____	21. 216 x 6 = ____
22. 305 x 7 = ____	23. 464 x 5 = ____	24. 441 x 9 = ____
25. 327 x 7 = ____	26. 453 x 6 = ____	27. 367 x 4 = ____

28. **267** coal trucks each made **8** trips to deliver coal to the port. How many trips to move the coal altogether? _______

29. Screws are boxed in lots of **144.** How many screws in seven boxes? _______

30. There are **9** bon-bons in each of **238** packs. How many bon-bons altogether? _______

31. **157** seats in each of nine rows. How many seats in total? _____

32. Fill in the missing numbers.

_____ 27, 29, 26, 28, 25, 27_____ _____

33. What is the special name for **144?**

____

1. 6) 750

2. 3) 222

3. 2) 620

4. 4) 924

5. 5) 885

6. 7) 672

7. 9) 963

8. 8) 768

9. 5) 865

10. **846** raffle tickets are to be sold in books of **6.** How many books of tickets? ______

11. **312** truck loads of sand are delivered to a building site. **8** trucks do the job. How many trips for each truck? ______

12. There are **516** children to travel on **6** buses. How many children on each bus? ______

13. David had **745** fish to move to **5** large ponds. If each pond holds the same number, how many in each pond? ______

14. **636** scones packed in batches of **12.** How many batches? ______

15. 2) 631 r

16. 4) 973 r

17. 9) 561 r

18. 7) 820 r

19. 5) 614 r

20. 9) 197 r

21. Mark all the co-ordinates on the grid, then join them to make a sailing boat picture.

J5 H5 H6 C5 G5 C1 C8
B1 B5 B8 A2 A6

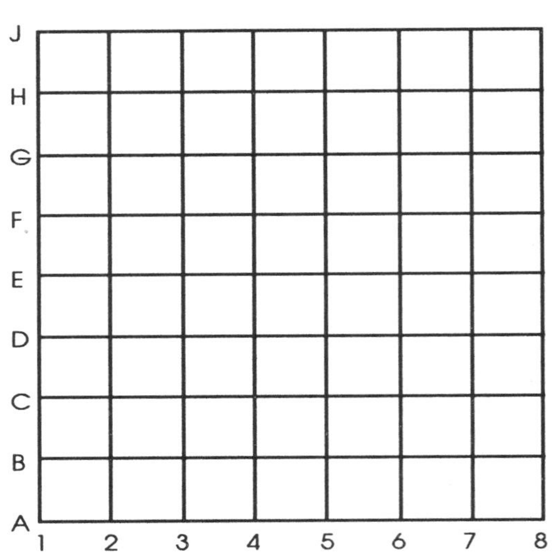

This is a map of Harper.

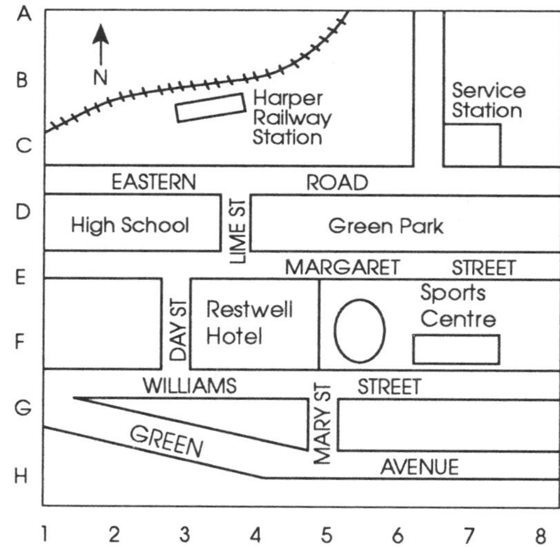

22. Give the co-ordinates of the railway station. ______

23. Give the co-ordinates of Restwell Hotel. ______

24. What are the co-ordinates for the northern end of Day St? ______

25. Give the co-ordinates where Green Ave and Williams Street meet. ______

Measure the **weight** of these items to the nearest **gram.**

1. 

_______ g

2. _______ g

3. 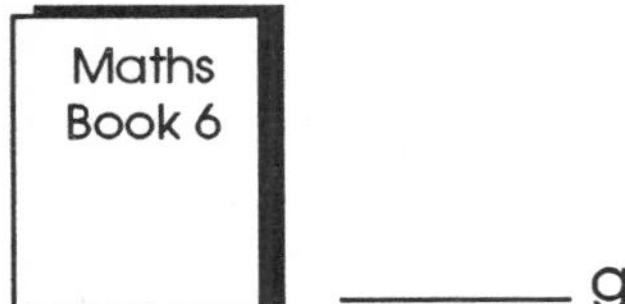

_______ g

4.  

_______ g

5. Find the weight of a milk carton filled with rice. _______

6. Find the weight of a milk carton filled with sand. _______

7. Find the weight of a glass jam jar. _______

8. What is the weight of the same jam jar filled with water? _______

9. What is the weight of the water? _______

10. What is the capacity of the jam jar in millilitres (ml)? _______

11. Complete this table.

Grams	Kilograms and Grams	Decimal Form
560		
		3.754kg
	7kg 250g	

Give the total **weight** of these as decimals.

12. 3kg + 700kg + 2kg + 690g = _______

13. 4kg + 4kg + 400g + 40g = _______

14. (3 x 3kg) + 13kg + 930g + 60g = _______

15. 5kg + (3 x 90g) + 72kg + $kg = _______

16. 6)493 r

17. 8)921 r

18. 5)647 r

19. 9)731 r

20. 8)685 r

21. 7)256 r

Find packaged supermarket items with these **net** (packed) weights. List them.

22. 50g _______________________

23. 200g _______________________

24. 250g _______________________

25. 500g _______________________

26. 1kg _______________________

27. You weigh a Rice-pops pack and find it has a weight of **535g.** The label says **Net wt. 525g.** What is the weight of the container? _______

28. A pickle jar has a weight of **517g,** but the label shows **net 310g.** What is the weight of the container? _______

Write these weights as decimals.

29. 9kg 476g _______

30. 14kg 35g _______

31. 5kg 600g _______

32. 8kg 8g _______

Write these weights as grams.

33. 5kg 28g _______

34. 25kg 52g _______

35. There are **567** razor blades to be packed in dispensers of **7.** How many dispensers can be filled? _______

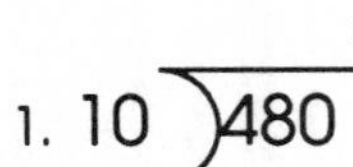

1. 10) 480 r 2. 10) 320 r 3. 10) 910 r

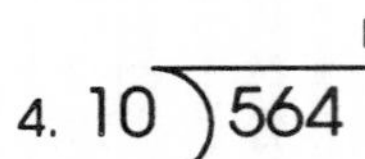

4. 10) 564 r 5. 10) 317 r 6. 10) 204 r

7. 10) 841 r 8. 10) 609 r 9. 10) 955 r

10. **252** dominoes have to be packed into **9** boxes. How many in each box? _______

11. **432** playing cards have to be packed in **8** boxes. How many cards in each box? _______

12. A roll of string 518 metres long is cut into seven equal pieces. How long is each piece? _______

13. **279** litres of water to fill 9 tanks. How many litres in each tank? _______

14. A company paid a bonus of **£947** to its **6** staff. How many whole pounds does each person receive? _______

15. Was there any money left over in question 14? If so, how much?

_______ £_______

16. Complete the division table.

÷	253	165	827	318	262
7	r	r	r	r	r
5	r	r	r	r	r

17. Colour the **3-D objects** that can be packed so there are no spaces between.

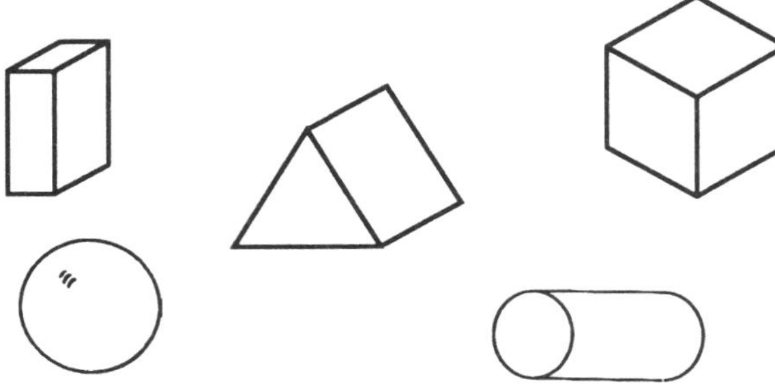

18. Give the total number of cubes in each of these **stacks.**

(a)

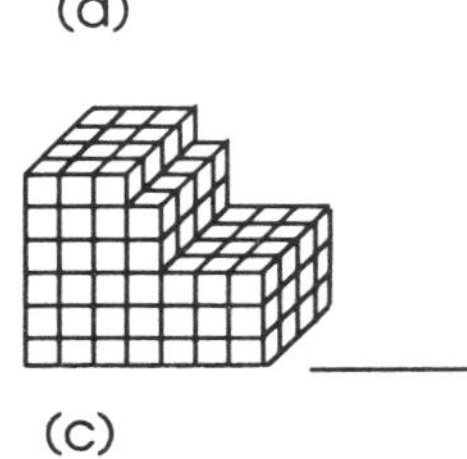

____

(b)

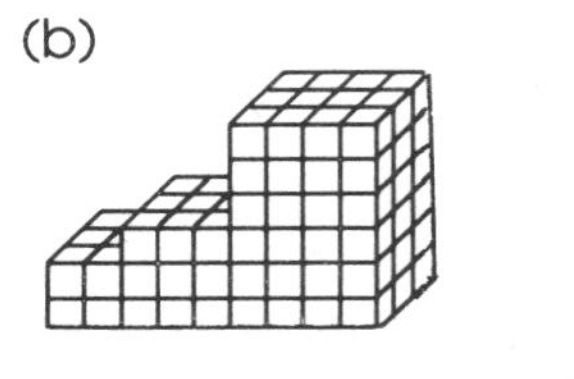

____

(c)

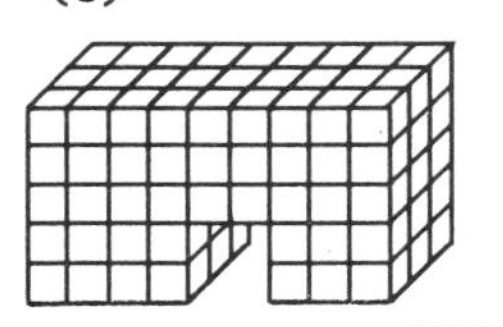

____

(d)

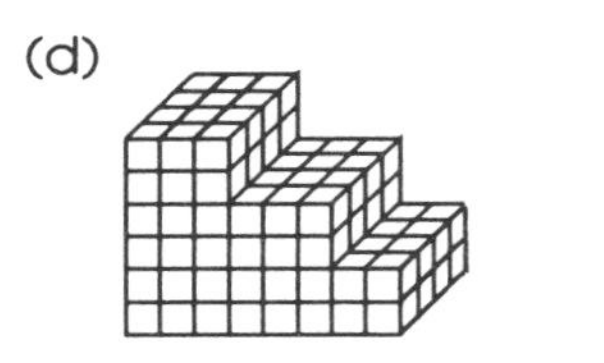

____

19. Look at these **stacks,** then work out how many more each needs to turn them into **solid stacks** with straight edges.

(a)

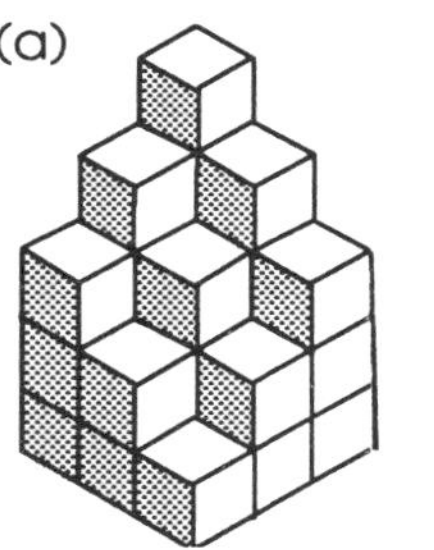

____

(b)

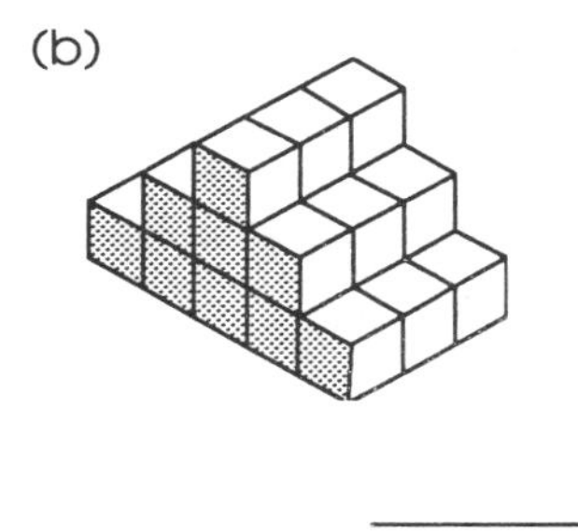

____

20. Draw a **container** suitable for packing six **cones** like this one.

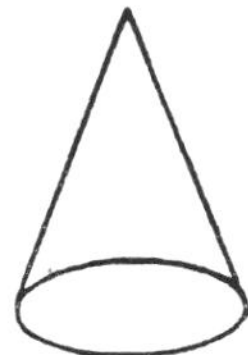

Here is a programme for a day at a camp.

Time	Activities	24hr Time
7.00 a.m.	Rise and shower	
8.15 a.m.	Breakfast	
9.20 a.m.	Nature walk	
11.00 a.m.	Morning break	
11.25 a.m.	Free time	
12.20 p.m.	Lunch	
1.35 p.m.	Film show	
2.45 p.m.	Conservation talk	
3.30 p.m.	Athletics competition	
5.00 p.m.	Free time	
5.45 p.m.	Dinner	
7.15 p.m.	Campfire	
8.40 p.m.	Supper	
9.30 p.m.	Lights out	

1. Write the 24 hour time for each activity in the programme.

2. How long between rising and lunch? ________

3. How long between morning tea break and the start of the campfire? ________

4. How long is the programme from rising to lights out? ________

5. A leaders' meeting was held at 1720. What p.m. time is this? ________

6. The nature-walk couldn't take place due to rain at 0445. Write this as a.m. or p.m. time. ________

Write these times in **24 hour** form.

7. Quarter past eleven at night. ________

8. Nineteen minutes to midday. ________

9. Forty-five minutes after midnight. ________

10. Twenty to six at twilight. ________

11. Show on this drawing how you would add four cubes to the stack.

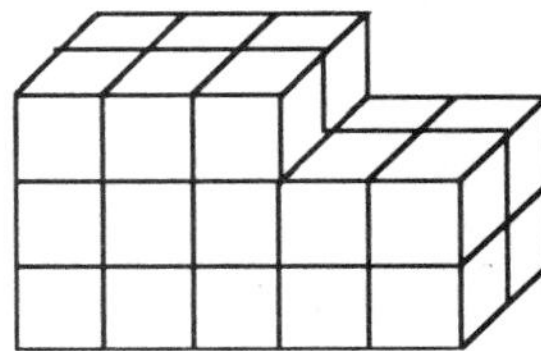

12. How many cubes altogether in the new stack? ________

13. These **cylinders** are very fragile. Design a foam package or box so they will not break.

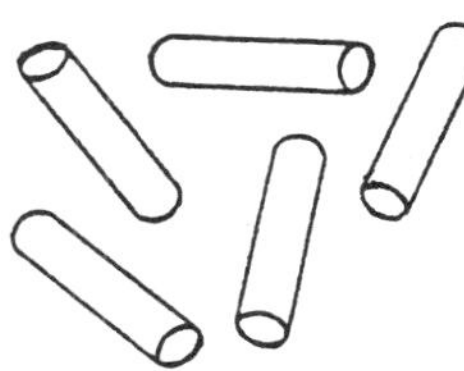

14. 10) 530 r

15. 10) 436 r

16. 10) 701 r

17. 10) 328 r

18. 10) 990 r

19. 10) 107 r

All the following times refer to the same day.

20. How long between 9.15 a.m. and 1.05 p.m.? ________

21. How long between 2.30 p.m. and 11.05 p.m.? ________

22. It is 4.14 p.m. but the clock says 1.57 p.m. How slow is it? ________

23. How long between 1040 hours and 1410 hours? ________

24. It is Christmas Day. It is 1500 hours. It is very dark. Where could I be?

____

Unit 29

Colour parts of each shape to match the **fraction.**

1. $\frac{1}{4}$
2. $\frac{1}{2}$
3. $\frac{7}{8}$
4. $\frac{1}{6}$
5. $\frac{3}{7}$
6. $\frac{1}{5}$

Colour parts of each group to match the **fraction.**

7. $\frac{3}{8}$
8. $\frac{7}{10}$
9. $\frac{4}{5}$
10. $\frac{3}{4}$
11. $\frac{2}{3}$

12. Fill in the table of **fractions, decimals** and **percentages.**

Fraction	Decimal	Percentage
$\frac{1}{2}$	0.5	50%
$\frac{1}{4}$		
$\frac{3}{4}$		
$\frac{1}{5}$		
$\frac{3}{5}$		
$\frac{1}{3}$		
$\frac{7}{10}$		

Change these **kilometres** to **metres.**

13. 16.85km ______________
14. 24.06km ______________
15. 19.91km ______________
16. 30.072km ______________
17. 6.003km ______________

Change these **metres** to **kilometres.**

18. 892m ______________
19. 24 783m ______________
20. 15 055m ______________
21. 3 303m ______________
22. 6m ______________

A map has a **scale** of **1cm = 1km.**

23. What would 12cm on the map be in **kilometres** on the ground? ________
24. What would 9.7cm on the map be in **kilometres** on the ground? ________
25. If you know the distance between two railway stations is 4km, what would be the distance on the map? ________
26. A national park on the map is 5cm x 5cm x 4cm x 5.5cm. What is the perimeter of the park in **km?** ________
27. If a road measuring 15cm can be made shorter by 3.5km by cutting a tunnel, what would it then measure on the map? ________
28. A road measures 16.5cm but a short cut on the map reduces the distance by 3km. How far will I travel, taking the short cut? ________

Fill in the **fractions.**

1. A theatre holds **100** people, but only **57** seats were taken for a concert. What fraction is this? _______

2. The **fraction** of vacant seats was? _______

3. Janine had one dozen oranges, but **3** dropped through a hole in the bag. What fraction was left? _______

4. Two chocolates were taken out of a box of **10.** What **fraction** of the box was left? _______

5. Sixteen veteran cars took part in a rally, but six broke down. What **fraction** finished the rally? _______

6. There were **20** goldfish in a tank, but **10** died. What **%** were left? _______

7. A pool was filled with 100 litres of water. During the day 29 litres leaked away. What percentage was left? _______

8. A radio/cassette usually sold for £100. It was discounted to £75. This was a discount of _______%

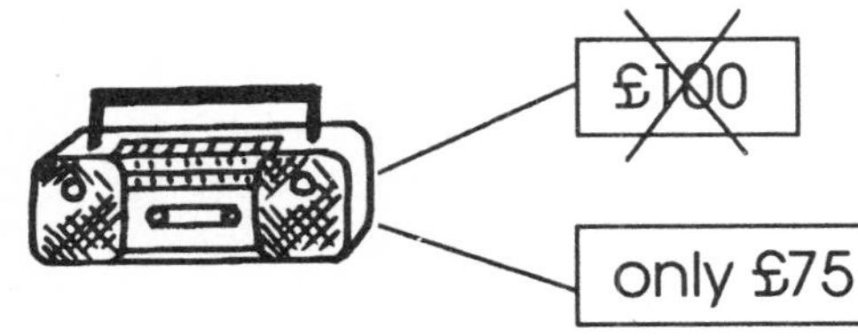

9. A video game usually sells for £40, but there is a sale and it sells for £30. What % discount is this? _______

10. 25% of £200 _______

11. 50% of 720 marbles _______

12. 75% of £1 000 _______

13. Shade **half** of this kite.

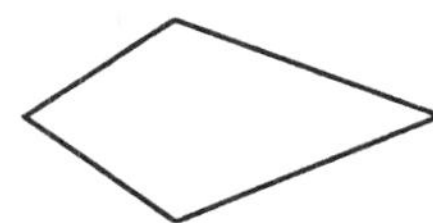

14. Shade **three quarters** of this circle.

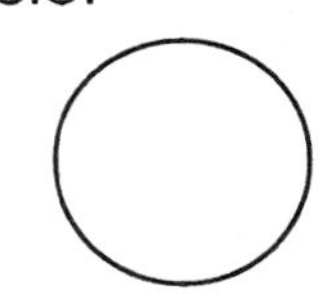

15. Colour **half** the triangle.

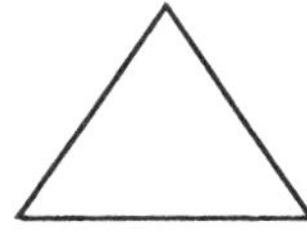

16. Shade $\frac{1}{8}$ of this octagon.

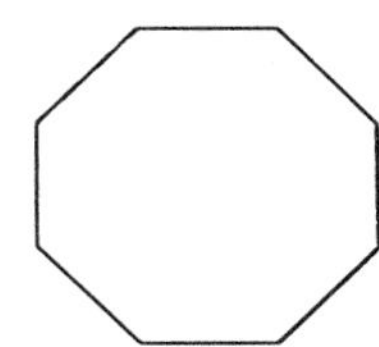

17. Shade 3 of this hexagon.

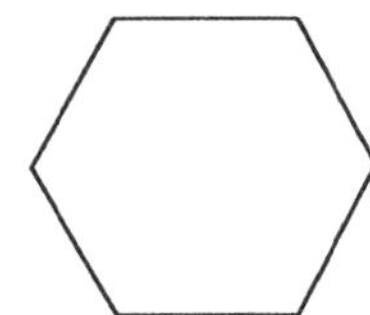

18. Divide this rectangle into **fifths,** then shade $\frac{3}{5}$.

19. Express $\frac{2}{5}$ as a **percentage.** _______

20. What is 0.75 as a **fraction?** _______

21. What is 20% as a **fraction?** _______

22. Write 80% in **decimal** form. _______

23. How many **metres** in 9.23km? _______

24. How many **metres** in 12.706km? _______

25. How many **kilometres** in 570m? _______

26. How many **kilometres** in 29 304m? _______

27. Complete the subtraction and percentage web. One is done for you.

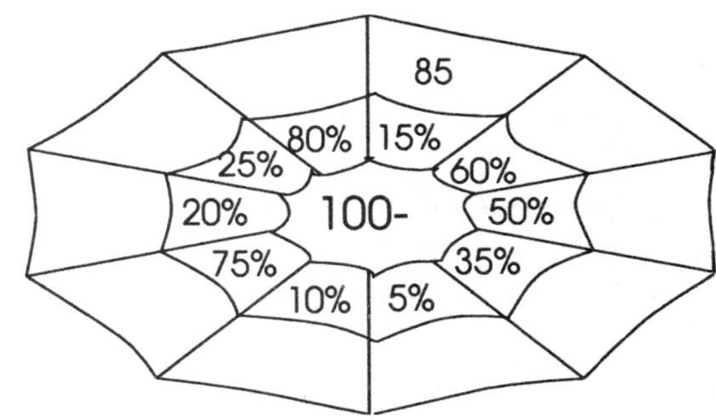

This is a bill from a greengrocery shop.

TED'S FRUIT
& VEG

	£
Cabbage	0.55
Bananas Lge	0.95
Brussels Sprouts	0.60
Melon	1.35
Tomatoes	1.70
Cauliflower	0.85
Celery	0.40
Potatoes	2.25
Oranges	1.35

Total: _______

Cash: _______

Change: _______

1. Find the total amount spent. _______

2. Fill in £20 opposite CASH.
   What is the change? _______

3. If Ted offers 10% off all items, what would the new total be? _______

4. What would bananas, celery and melon cost if only these were bought? _______

5. Which would cost more, melon and tomatoes or potatoes and cauliflower? _______

6. What would 4 cabbages cost? _______

7. If the bananas, oranges and potatoes were returned, what would be the refund? _______

8. Find out about 'old money'.
   (a) How many pennies made one shilling? _______
   (b) How many shillings in a pound? _______

9. Pack these items into the plastic bag, and in a few words explain why you packed it that way.

____

____

____

10. List two or three items you buy in the supermarket that have these shapes.
   (a) cylinder: _______________________
   (b) sphere: _______________________
   (c) cube: _______________________
   (d) rectangular based prism: _______________________
   (e) cone: _______________________
   (f) square based prism: _______________________
   (g) any type of pyramid: _______________________

Write in **hectares,** using decimal form.

1. 35 000 square metres ____________
2. 137 000 square metres ____________
3. 275 000 square metres ____________
4. 86 500 square metres ____________
5. 65 000 square metres ____________

6. Draw a plan of a 28 hectare farm. Use $1cm^2$ to represent 1 hectare.

7. Work out the **area,** in **hectares,** of the land your school stands on. ______

8. Work out the **area,** in **square metres,** that your home stands on. ______

9. A housing estate is **10 hectares.** Fifty houses are built on it, each with an area of $600m^2$. What area remains for roads and open land? ______

10. Add these areas and write the answers as **hectares.**

(a) $15\,000m^2$, $25\,000m^2$ and $75\,000m^2$ _____

(b) $35\,000m^2$, $65\,000m^2$ and $50\,000m^2$ _____

(c) $18\,000m^2$, $92\,000m^2$ and $35\,000m^2$ _____

(d) $27\,000m^2$, $21\,500m^2$ and $85\,500m^2$ _____

11. A supermarket is offering 25% off all these items. Write the new prices.

GREAT BONANZA SALE

	Price	Discount Price
Fruit Cake	£1.60	____
Oat Bran	£1.80	____
Sausages	£2.40	____
Cheese	£2.80	____
Chicken	£4.40	____
	TOTAL:	____
	CASH:	____
	CHANGE:	____

12. At the **discount prices** what would oat bran, cheese and chicken cost altogether? ______

13. What is the total of all amounts before **discount** ? ______

14. Write in the total of **discount** prices.

15. Write £20 in CASH, then work out and write in the **change.**

16. What is the difference between the usual and **discount prices?** ______

17. Which cost more, fruit cake and cheese, or chicken? ______

Change these to **hectares.**

18. $12\,640m^2$ ______ 19. $17\,358m^2$ ______

20. $29\,006m^2$ ______ 21. $62\,175m^2$ ______

22. Can you think of a large object that is the shape of a **cylinder**?

____

23. How many **hectares**?

$13\,000m^2 + 9\,000m^2 + 18\,000m^2$ ______

Unit 31

1.
```
  1306
  4728
+  659
```

2.
```
  2762
  7901
+ 3528
```

3.
```
  1374
  5722
+ 8963
```

4.
```
  7043
  5838
    17
+ 9620
```

5.
```
   243
  3044
  4303
+   12
```

6.
```
  3403
   304
  4030
+  344
```

Fill in the gaps.

7.
```
  493_
  70_5
+ 2762
 14_58
```

8.
```
  913_
  80_7
+ _356
 20_04
```

9.
```
  8_76
  12_7
+ _409
 13952
```

10. Add together the total for questions 7, 8 and 9. Write and complete the **sum**. +

Add the sums of money.

11.
```
 £6831.21
  7410.37
+ 3255.46
```

12.
```
 £5213.19
  4562.67
+ 2018.41
```

13.
```
 £2163.48
+ 4192.73
```

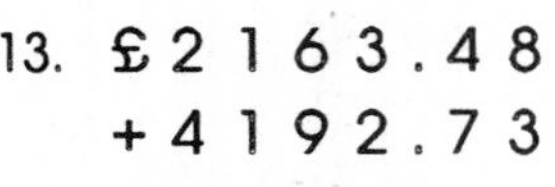

14.
```
 £6543.81
+ 2798.89
```

15. Cut these shapes out of card. With a torch, in a darkened room, vary the angle of the torch or shape to make different shadows. Draw some of them here.

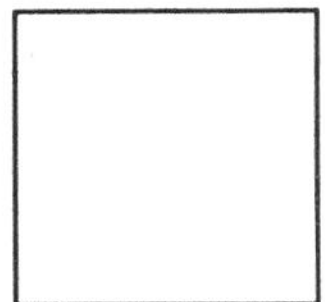

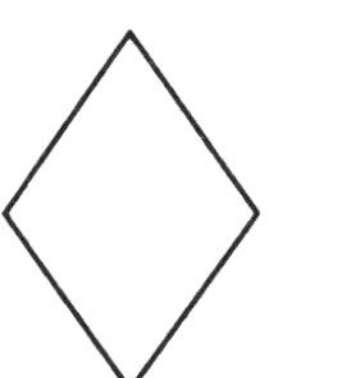

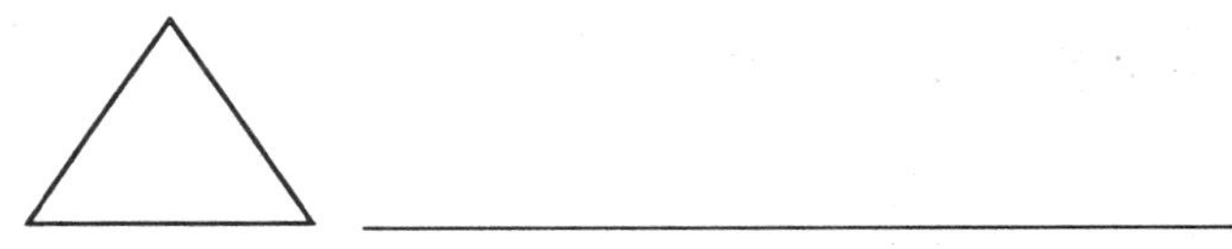

A car salesman listed his sales of 6 cars during the week.

	£
SLEEKA SPORTS	16 110
MINIMOTO	10 715
4WD BUSHRANGER	18 700
FAMILY DELITE	10 385
DIESEL DUMP	17 212
EAGLE	13 000
	______

1. What did his sales total? ____________

2. He had an inquiry about the sale of 4 Minimotos. What would the sale be worth? ____________

3. He missed the sale of another 4WD Bushranger because he could not give 10% discount. What would the price have been? ________

4. The family that bought the DELITE received £5 000 trade-in on their old car. What did they have to pay in cash? ____________

5. The builder who bought the DIESEL DUMP added a bull bar (£260), air conditioning (£1 005) and fog lights (£147). What price did he pay altogether? ____________

6. The woman who bought the EAGLE paid £10 000 in cash. She will have to pay 20% interest for the first year on the balance. How much will this be? ________

7.
```
  3471
   382
+ 4758
------
```

8.
```
   674
  5039
+ 1608
------
```

9.
```
  4070
  3149
+ 6432
------
```

10.
```
  7164
  4258
+ 9574
------
```

11.
```
  8040
  1386
+ 5457
------
```

12.
```
  2713
  6279
+ 1456
------
```

13. What shadow would each of these **3-D** objects make?

(a)

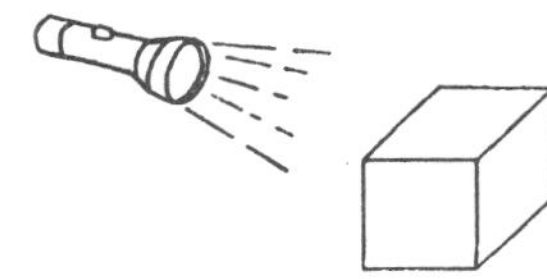

(b)

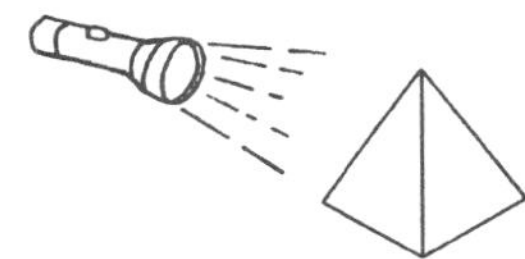

14.
```
   30_3
   7286
+  _081
-------
  15440
```

15.
```
   _340
    76_
+  8218
-------
  18_20
```

16.
```
   10_0
   7063
+  _102
-------
  1720_
```

Add the money.

17.
```
£  491.25
  2067.42
+ 6140.27
---------
```

18.
```
£ 7963.74
  8150.33
+ 6298.65
---------
```

Unit 32

1. 383 − 28 = ____

2. 461 − 30 = ____

3. 274 − 93 = ____

4. 506 − 72 = ____

5. 854 − 57 = ____

6. 505 − 18 = ____

Fill in the missing numbers.

7. 29_ − 15 = 279

8. _08 − 44 = 564

9. 503 − 18 = _85

10. 71_ − _9 = _02

11. _70 − 6_ = 4_9

12. __2 − 63 = 479

13. Of 375 children in a piano competition, only 89 reached the finals. How many dropped out? ________

14. A man had £794 in the bank at the end of January. A month later he had £58. How much had he spent? ________

15. A trip was 780 km. The sign post said only 175 km to go. How far had I travelled? ________

16. 463 − 157 = ____

17. 386 − 179 = ____

18. 843 − 677 = ____

19. The mountaineer is standing in front of a high mountain - yet it looks smaller than he is. Explain this.

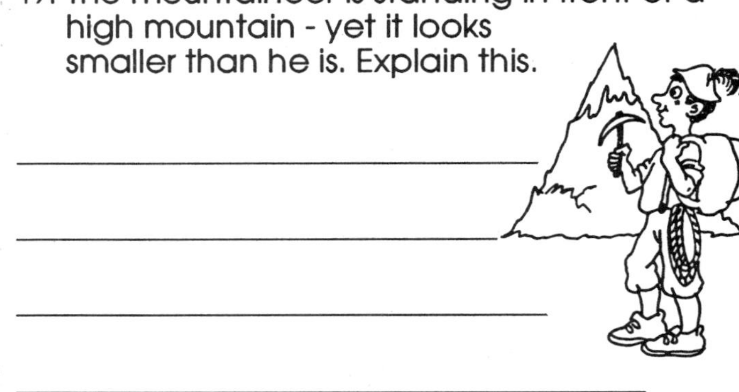

____

____

____

____

20. Draw more of the road up the page, to its **vanishing point**.

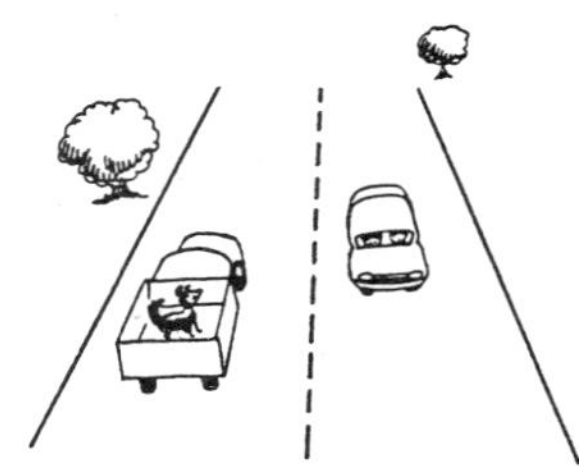

21. Finish the picture so the **perspective** is correct.

22. Could it be true that these pylons are the same height? Explain.

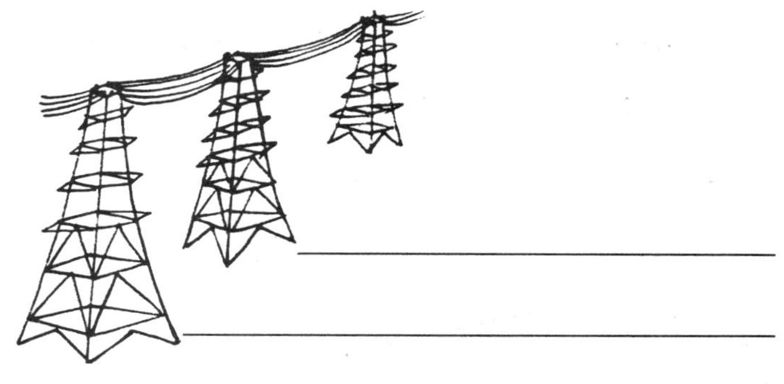

____

____

____

Choose the more appropriate unit of capacity, **cm^3** or **m^3**, for each of the following.

1. A box containing a doll. ________
2. Kitchen waste container. ________
3. A container like those carried by ships and trains. ________
4. A shop's drink refrigerator. ________
5. The cargo hold of a ship. ________
6. The boot of a car. ________
7. A chocolate box. ________
8. Use bathroom scales to measure your weight. ________
9. Hold a heavy object in your hand and weigh yourself again. ______
10. What is the weight of the object? ________
11. Measure the weight of another family member or friend. ________
12. Weigh your schoolbag packed for school. ________
13. Find a truck or tanker with **gross weight** printed on it. Record it here.

    Gross weight ___________

14. What does **gross weight** mean?

    ____

    ____

15. Explain how you can find the weight of water in a glass, using scales twice only.

    ____

    ____

16. 429 − 63 = ______
17. 578 − 39 = ______
18. 741 − 55 = ______
19. 898 − 89 = ______
20. 657 − 78 = ______
21. 625 − 179 = ______

Fill in the missing numbers.

22. 31_ − 67 = 251
23. _72 − 5_ = 419
24. 88_ − 47 = _36

Use kitchen **scales** or bathroom **scales** to find these **weights**.

25. A house brick ________
26. A saucepan ________
27. A cushion ________
28. A suitcase packed with clothes ready for a journey. ________
29. A small stool or footrest. ________
30. An airline has a **luggage limit** of **40kg** per passenger. If you were taking your suitcase (Q28) would you:

- Be about right? ☐
- Be allowed to take twice as much? ☐
- Be allowed to take three times as much? ☐
- Be allowed to take four times as much? ☐

31. ___ − 624 = 217
32. 645 − ___ = 158
33. _6_ − 3_4 = 245

1. 348 − 140	2. 274 − 155	3. 687 − 419
4. 851 − 707	5. 657 − 226	6. 669 − 897

Complete the **subtraction** wheel.

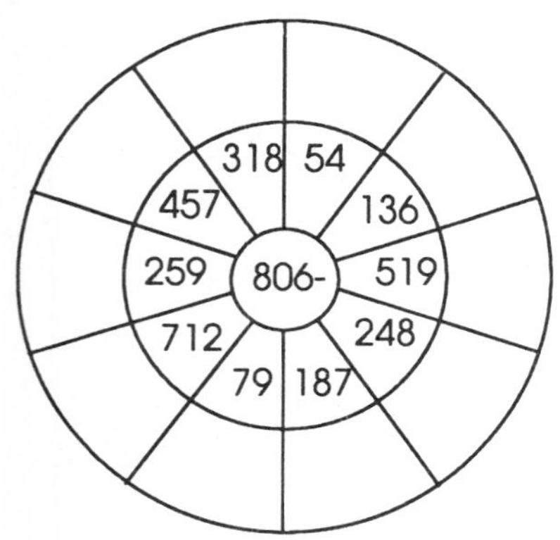

8. Four hundred and forty small pine trees are felled from a forest of 759. How many left? ______

9. It takes the planet Pluto 247 years to circle the sun. It takes Uranus 164 years. What is the difference in years? ______

10. Fill in the **subtraction** train.

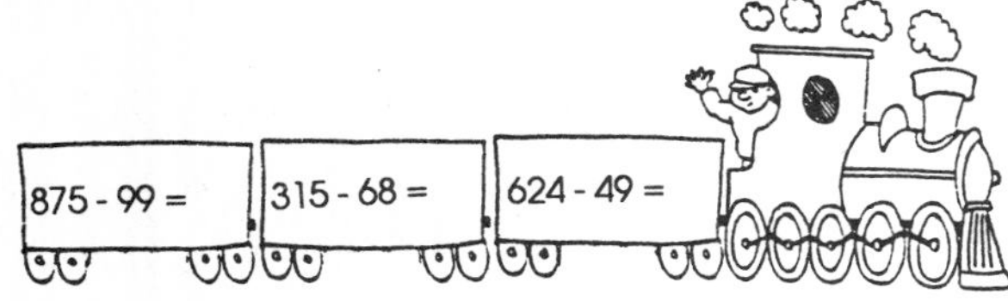

11. There were 975 passengers on a train. At one stop 87 got off and at the next 65. How many were left on the train? ______

12. There were 685 sheep on a farm. 196 were taken to an auction and 153 to the market. How many sheep were left? ______

This is a map of the city of Harper.

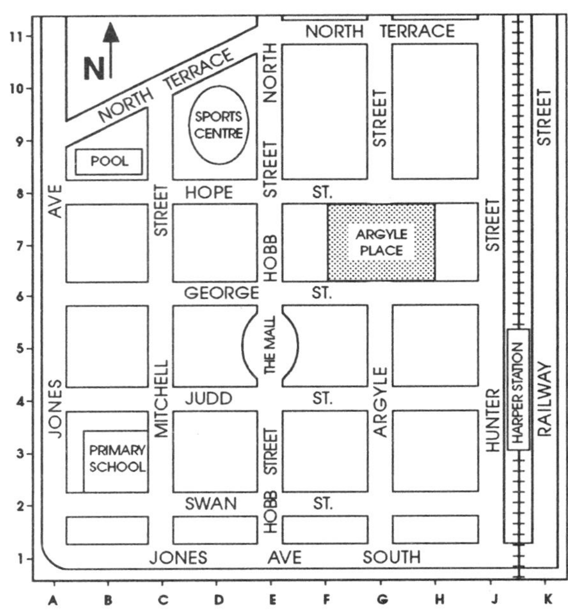

13. What streets meet at E8? ______

14. What streets meet at C4? ______

15. What is at E5? ______

16. Give the co-ordinates for these:

(a) Argyle St and Judd St. ______

(b) George St and Hunter St. ______

(c) Jones Ave and Hope St. ______

(d) North Terrace and Mitchell St. ______

17. What is the square bordered by F6, F8, H8 and H6? ______

18. Give references for where North Terrace begins and ends on the map. ______

19. In the alphabet part of the grid, why has the letter I been left out?

______

1. Estimate what the **temperature** is now. ______

2. Use a **thermometer** to measure the **temperature** it is now. ______

3. How many degrees out were you? ______

4. Here is a table of **maximum** and **minimum** temperatures over 7 days. Fill in the missing figures.

Days of the week	Min	Max	Difference
Sunday	7°C	15°C	
Monday	9°C		14°C
Tuesday		21°C	12°C
Wednesday	10°C		13°C
Thursday	4°C	27°C	
Friday	6°C	31°C	
Saturday		33°C	23°C

Arrange the **temperatures** in order, lowest to highest.

5. 19°C 27°C 39°C 11°C 68°C 8°C

______

6. 72°C 48°C 51°C 25°C 17°C 34°C

______

7. Mark the temperatures on the **Celsius** thermometers.

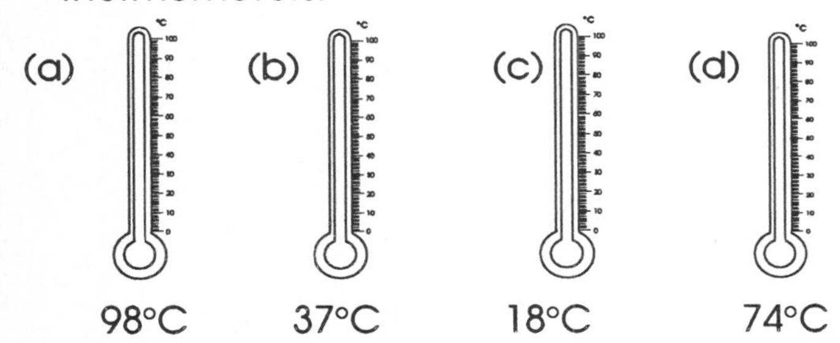

98°C 37°C 18°C 74°C

8. Find out what **absolute zero** temperature is in **degrees Celsius**. ______

9. 684 − 260 = ______

10. 531 − 222 = ______

11. 497 − 364 = ______

12. 709 − 483 = ______

13. 842 − 573 = ______

14. 904 − 711 = ______

15. 257 − 169 = ______

16. 897 − 798 = ______

17. 904 − 149 = ______

18. Seven hundred and fifty seats were available for a football match. 619 were pre-sold; 24 were reserved for club officials. How many were left? ______

19. There are 257 children at a sports day. One hundred and sixteen are under nine years of age. How many are over nine? ______

20. 473 teddy bears went to the teddy bears' picnic. 157 were disqualified for not being true teddies. How many true teddies were there? ______

21. There are four gross (1 gross = 144) of jellybeans in a jar. Half a gross are green; two gross are red. How many are other colours? ______

22. Write the **temperatures** in **rising** order.

46°C 39°C 14°C 8°C 33°C 50°C

______

23. Write the **temperatures** in **falling** order.

72°C 31°C 47°C 29°C 16°C 18°C

______

1. 348 × 8 = ______

2. 293 × 9 = ______

3. 423 × 5 = ______

4. 567 × 4 = ______

5. 908 × 2 = ______

6. 1764 × 3 = ______

7. 2091 × 4 = ______

8. 3635 × 3 = ______

9. 4382 × 4 = ______

10. Complete this **multiplication** fan.

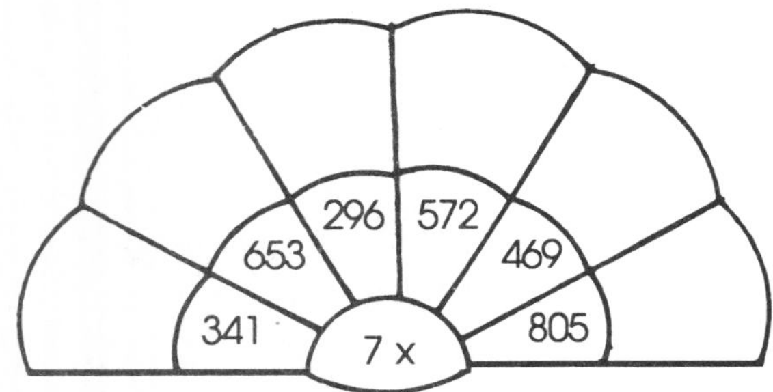

11. Four groups of 1750 soldiers landed on the beach at Gallipoli. How many soldiers in total? ______

12. One thousand three hundred and fifty-six kilograms of wheat in each silo. How many kilograms in 7 silos? ______

13. Eight farms with 2 375 sheep on each. How many sheep? ______

14. Complete this **multiplication** fan.

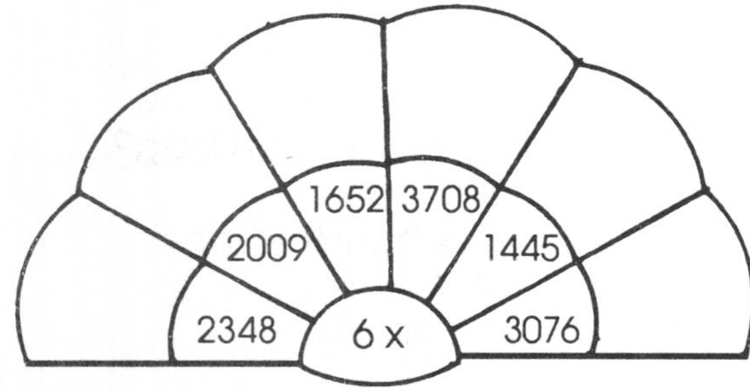

15. Read, then write the **minutes** and **seconds** shown on each stopwatch.

(a) 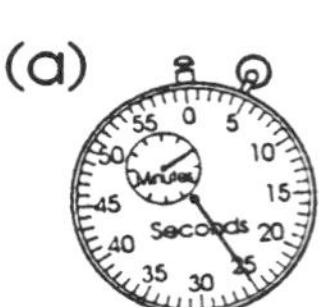

______

(b) ______

(c) 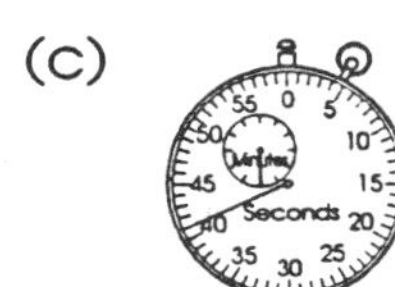

______

(d) 0:24 Stopwatch ______

(e) 9:49 Stopwatch ______

(f) 2:03 Stopwatch ______

16. With a friend, each with a watch or stopwatch, record these times. Then write the differences.

Activity	My time	Friend's time	Difference
Count 1 to 100			
Write name and address			
Write the alphabet			
Count a pack of cards			
Touch toes 20 times			
Read page of a book aloud			

17. Why are there differences in time for the activities above?

______

______

These times are in hours, minutes and seconds. Write them out in full.

18. 3:10:52 ______

19. 14:25:10 ______

20. 0:45:35 ______

1. 3) 392 r
2. 6) 461 r
3. 4) 515 r
4. 5) 278 r
5. 2) 351 r
6. 7) 564 r
7. 8) 731 r
8. 6) 697 r
9. 5) 777 r
10. 7) 583 r

11. **560** children were to travel on **7** buses to a concert. How many on each bus? ________

How many left over? ________

12. **£791** was shared evenly among **6** people. Money that was not an even share was used to buy raffle tickets. How much did each receive? ________

13. How much was left for raffle tickets? ________

14. Share **879** among **9**. Record the remainder as well. ______r___

15. 3) 8172 r
16. 6) 6874 r
17. 4) 5131 r
18. 5) 4627 r
19. 7) 834 r
20. 6) 2733 r

21. 1636 x 4
22. 2780 x 5
23. 3106 x 6
24. 4828 x 7
25. 1053 x 8
26. 2530 x 9

27. Use a watch or stopwatch to find how long it takes a friend to count backwards from 100 to 1. ________

28. Look at a CD or tape to find a popular song. Write its name and how long the song plays.

________________________ ________

29. Some early clocks had only one hand. Which one would it have been? ________

30. Why was only one hand needed?

____

____

31. 3) 421 r
32. 6) 798 r
33. 4) 7092 r
34. 5) 4416 r

35. Seven thousand four hundred and fifty-nine coins are counted into 9 bags. How many in each bag? ________

36. Five thousand six hundred and seventy-six bulbs planted in eight beds. How many in each bed? ________

Unit 35

1. A head teacher divided **272** pupils in Years 6 and 7 into **8** equal classes. How many pupils in each class? _______

2. **£855** is to be divided into nine equal pay packets. How much in each? _______

3. A carpenter making **7** cabinets knows he has **329** screws to do the job. How many screws for each? _______

4. A saleswoman covered **928** km travelling between her home and the same town **8** times. How far is her home from the town? _______

5. Divide **793** oranges into bags of **10**. How many in each bag? _______

6. How many oranges left over in question 5? _______

7. **913** books are to be arranged on **7** library shelves in even numbers. How many on each shelf? _______

   How many left over? _______

8. $3\overline{)4316}$ r

9. $6\overline{)2845}$ r

10. $4\overline{)3782}$ r

11. $5\overline{)4791}$ r

12. $7\overline{)2417}$ r

13. $6\overline{)4927}$ r

14. A group of **357** people have to disembark from a ship. The launch can take **9** people at a time. How many trips? _______

This is a picture graph of gardening tools at a local hardware shop.

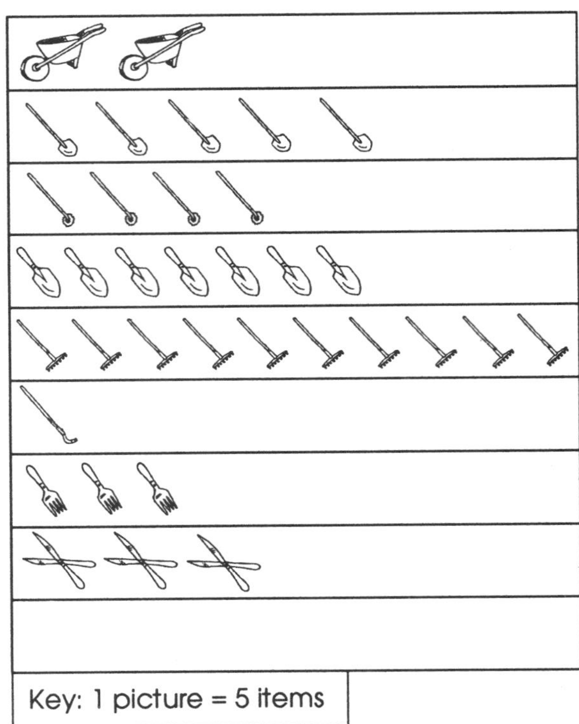

15. How many garden trowels in the store? _______

16. How many wheelbarrows? _______

17. How many rakes? _______

18. How many hedge clippers and edgers? _______

19. The manager decided he needed the same number of forks as spades. How many more forks did he order? _______

20. Wheelbarrows were **£30** less **10%** How much will they receive if they sell all the barrows? _______

21. During a stock take 10 more hoes were found. Adjust the graph.

22. Fifteen garden brooms were also found. Add them to the graph.

Order these **decimals** smallest to largest.

1. 0.4 0.2 0.3 0.7 0.1

___

2. 0.8 0.9 0.6 0.3 0.5

___

3. 1.3 1.9 2.3 0.8 1.7

___

4. 2.4 3.4 1.3 5.1 4.7

___

5. 1.7 7.1 2.8 8.2 7.8

___

Remove any **non-significant** (not needed) **zeros** in these **fractions**. Write them correctly.

6. 03.41 ___
7. 2.70 ___
8. 20.05 ___
9. 04.80 ___
10. 10.010 ___
11. 06.06 ___

Write these **centimetres** as **metres** in **decimal** form.

12. 147 cm ___
13. 36 cm ___
14. 509 cm ___
15. 960 cm ___
16. 4328 cm ___

Turn these pence into pounds, in **decimal** form.

17. 345p ___
18. 625p ___
19. 599p ___
20. 1755p ___

21. Draw a **picture graph** that shows these items from a cutlery drawer.

12 knives 10 forks 8 teaspoons
9 dessert spoons 3 big spoons

22. 7) 3 460 r
23. 6) 4 571 r
24. 8) 5 873 r
25. 4) 6 193 r
26. 9) 351 r
27. 6) 4 719 r
28. 7) 731 r
29. 10) 7 033 r

Write these amounts as **pence**.

30. £4.76 ___
31. £11.08 ___
32. £29.11 ___
33. £39. 87 ___
34. £107.01 ___
35. £257.62 ___

Write these **fractions**, removing the **non-significant zeros**.

36. 09.01 ___
37. 50.60 ___
38. 100.08 ___
39. 05.030 ___
40. 070.50 + 7.05 + 02.40 = ___

Unit 36

1. Arrange these numbers on two lines in order, smallest to largest.

37 856 19 241 58 027 83 452

48 375 62 717 59 320 8 916

____

____

Write the values of the numbers in bold.

2. 4**1** 683 ________________

3. 67 **2**51 ________________

4. **2**4 159 ________________

5. 53 27**3** ________________

Write these numbers in words.

6. 237 325 ________________________

7. 891 260 ________________________

8.
```
   275
   168
   319
 +  12
```

9.
```
   306
   145
   197
 + 208
```

10.
```
   2460
   7138
   5027
 + 3652
```

11.
```
 £2.64
  1.15
  3.59
 +1.77
```

12.
```
 £3.99
  0.45
  2.76
 +1.33
```

13.
```
 £173.21
   59.68
  341.72
 +  0.95
```

14. Four second hand cars sold for £4295, £6170, £3050 and £7465. How much altogether? ________

Label each angle **acute**, **obtuse**, **right angle**, **reflex** or **straight.** Then measure each angle using a protractor.

	Angle	Type of angle	Degrees
15.	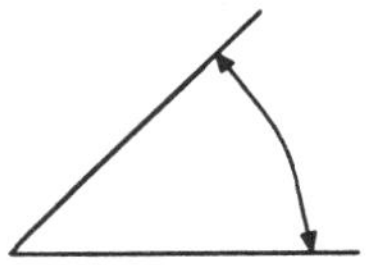		
16.	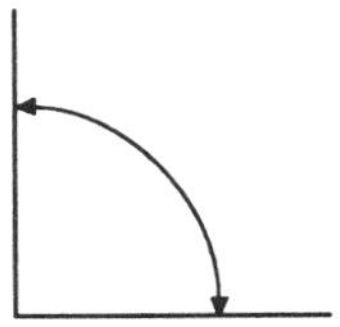		
17.	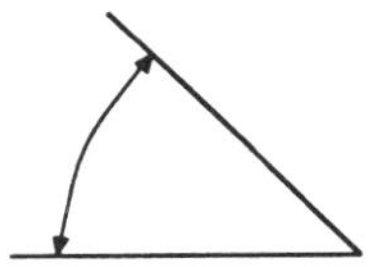		
18.	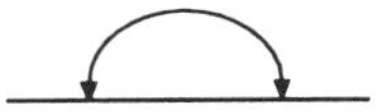		
19.	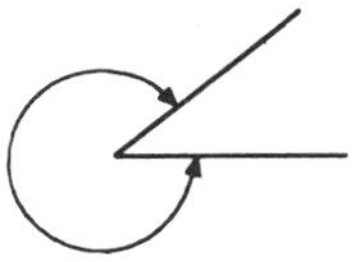		
20.			
21.	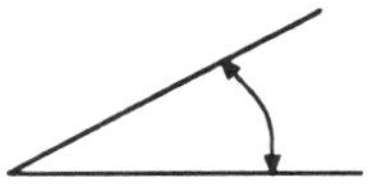		

1. Measure these lengths in **millimetres**.

(a) One side of a postage stamp ________

(b) The diameter of a 20p coin ________

(c) Circumference of a 50p coin ________

(d) Thickness of a £2 coin ________

(e) Length of a pen ________

(f) Length of your index finger ________

(g) Thickness of this book ________

(h) Length of a comb ________

2. Write these measurements in **centimetres** and **millimetres**. The first one is done for you.

(a) 255 mm = 25 cm 5 mm

(b) 318 mm = ________________

(c) 467 mm = ________________

(d) 111 mm = ________________

(e) 792 mm = ________________

(f) 1273 mm = ________________

3. Draw a circle with a **radius** of 27 mm.

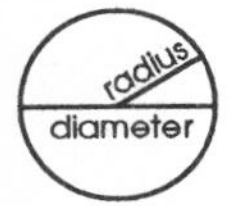

4. What is the circle's **diameter**? ________

5. What is the circumference in centimetres and millimetres? ________

6. Measure the angles.

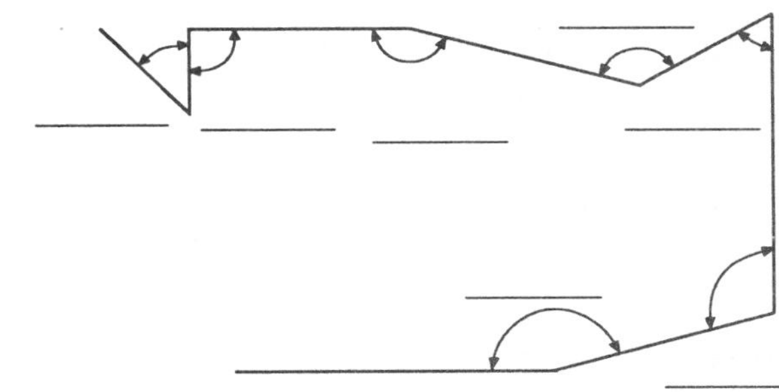

7.
```
   316
  2780
    15
+ 3060
------
```

8.
```
  7851
  5326
   493
+ 2032
------
```

9.
```
  1711
  2086
    14
+ 8953
------
```

Fill in the missing numbers.

10.
```
   3_42
   _665
+  571_
-------
  133_1
```

11.
```
   _761
   37__
+  2_85
-------
  14172
```

12.
```
   3162
   2_73
+  115_
-------
   _8_8
```

13. Measure the lines in **millimetres**.

(a) ________ mm

(b) ________ mm

(c) ________ mm

(d) ________ mm

Measure these objects in **millimetres**.

14. Paper clip ________ mm

15. Toothpick ________ mm

16. Width of a ruler ________ mm

17. Width of your thumbnail ________ mm

Write in **cm** and **mm**.

18. 854 mm ________________

19. 139 mm ________________

20. 682 mm ________________

1. 322 − 234 = ____

2. 495 − 343 = ____

3. 270 − 163 = ____

4. 587 − 328 = ____

5. 653 − 464 = ____

6. 861 − 286 = ____

Fill in the missing numbers.

7. 4 __ 8 − 1 8 9 = 2 3 __

8. 7 7 __ − 2 8 5 = __ 8 9

9. 6 __ 3 − 4 8 __ = 1 2 2

10. __ 3 9 − 5 __ 4 = 3 9 __

11. 8 __ 4 − 5 __ 8 = __ 7 6

12. 2 __ 7 − 1 __ = __ 7 9

13. Jade had £365 in the bank. She withdrew £219 leaving a balance of : ________

14. A week later Jade withdrew another £56. How much does she have left? ________

15. A chemist has 464 tubes of sunscreen. He sells 170 tubes. How many tubes does he have left? ________

16. Complete the subtraction flowers.

Using a **protractor**, draw these angles.

17. 80°

18. 25°

19. 60°

20. 100°

21. 40°

22. 120°

23. Look at the words and letters in these instructions carefully and **tally** the vowels (a,e,i,o,and u). Count y as a vowel too. Then make a **graph** of the tallies in an exercise book.

a	
e	
i	
o	
u	
y	

Draw these five rectangles on **one centimetre** squared grid paper and work out their area in **square centimetres**.

	Length	Width	Area
1.	2 cm	4 cm	
2.	3 cm	2 cm	
3.	5 cm	6 cm	
4.	6 cm	1 cm	
5.	5 cm	4 cm	

Without drawing them, work out the areas of these rectangles and squares.

	Length	Width	Area
6.	3 cm	6 cm	
7.	5 cm	7 cm	
8.	6 cm	6 cm	
9.	9 cm	9 cm	
10.	4 cm	9 cm	

Work out the areas of these shapes, by forming rectangles and squares. *(Not to scale.)*

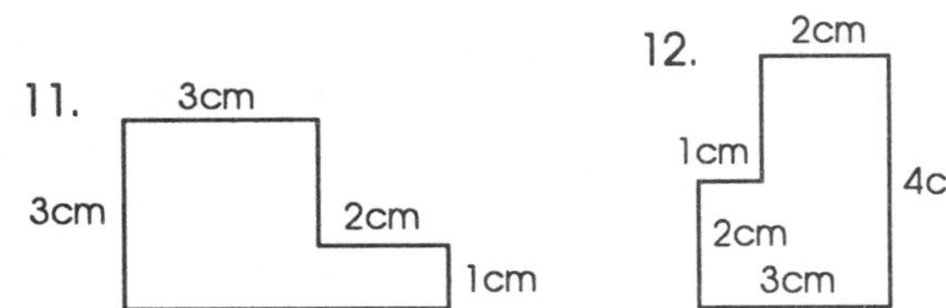

Area = ________ cm^2 Area = ________ cm^2

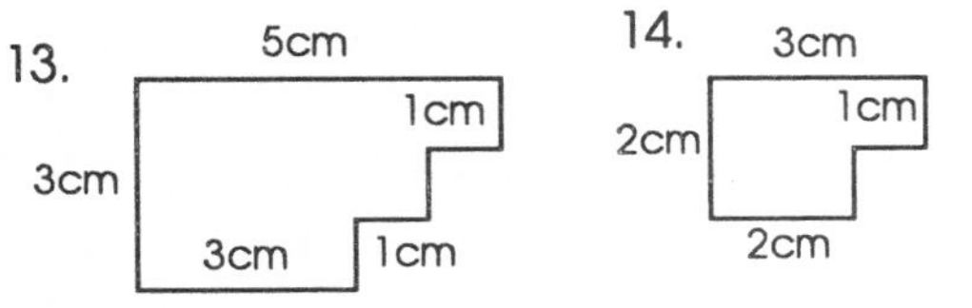

Area = ________ cm^2 Area = ________ cm^2

15. A badly printed book of 142 pages has only 113 pages with print on them. How many blank pages? ________

16. A girl scores 897 on a computer game. Her brother scores 638. What is the girl's winning margin? ________

17. 3 7 3 − 3 3 7 = ________

18. 9 5 4 − 4 4 5 = ________

19. 5 3 8 − 3 5 9 = ________

20. __ 0 2 − 2 1 7 = 3 8 __

21. 7 __ 7 − 3 7 __ = 3 4 9

22. 9 __ 3 − __ 0 4 = 2 8 __

23. Use a protractor to draw these angles.

(a) 45° ________

(b) 60° ________

(c) 90° ________

(d) 165° ________

(e) 115° ________

(f) 135° ________

24. Find the areas of these rectangles in cm^2.

(a) 8 cm x 10 cm = ________

(b) 7 cm x 9 cm = ________

(c) 6 cm x 14 cm = ________

(d) 9 cm x 15 cm = ________

1. Complete the **multiplication** number puzzle.

1. 7 x 76
2. 6 x 458
3. 5 x 91
4. 4 x 134
5. 9 x 42
6. 8 x 623
7. 9 x 107
8. 3 x 277

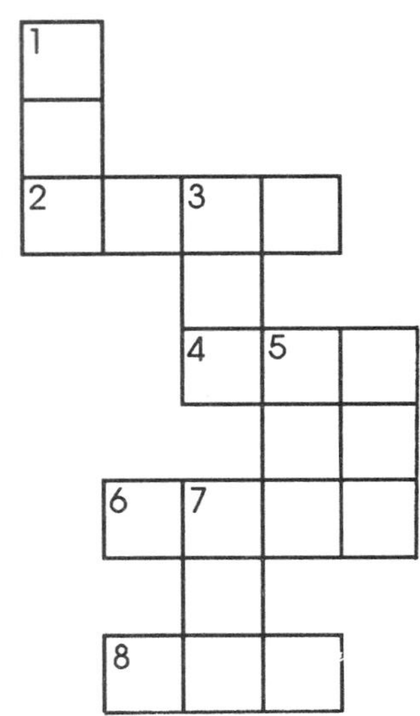

Use a calculator to help do these larger **multiplication** sums.

2. 4 x 6 483 = __________

3. 5 x 5 167 = __________

4. 7 x 3 964 = __________

5. 8 x 4 175 = __________

6. 6 x 6 277 = __________

7. 8) 748 r

8. 3) 596 r

9. 5) 634 r

10. 7) 8351 r

Complete these **division** sums.

11. 847 ÷ 4 = __________

12. 902 ÷ 7 = __________

13. 756 ÷ 6 = __________

14. 977 ÷ 9 = __________

This **graph** shows the profits of a company (in millions of pounds) over a period of 6 years.

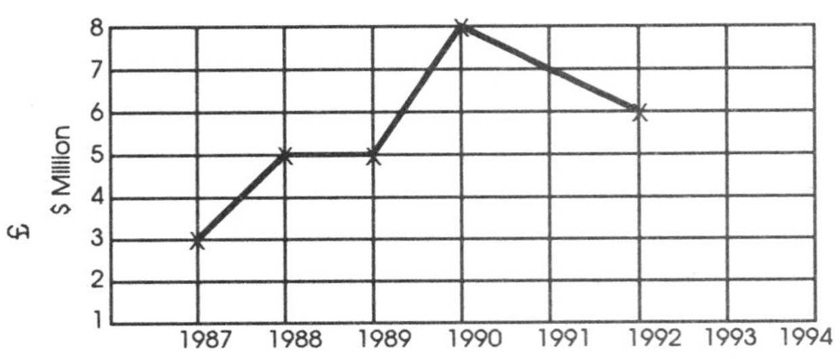

15. What was the company's profit in 1989? £______

16. How much did the annual profit rise between 1987 and 1992? £______

17. What was the company's total profit over six years? £______

18. The 1993 profit is only half that of 1992. Show this on the graph.

19. If the profit in 1994 is to be twice the 1987 profit, show this on the graph.

20. Here are three views of a **3-D** object. Draw it on the grid.

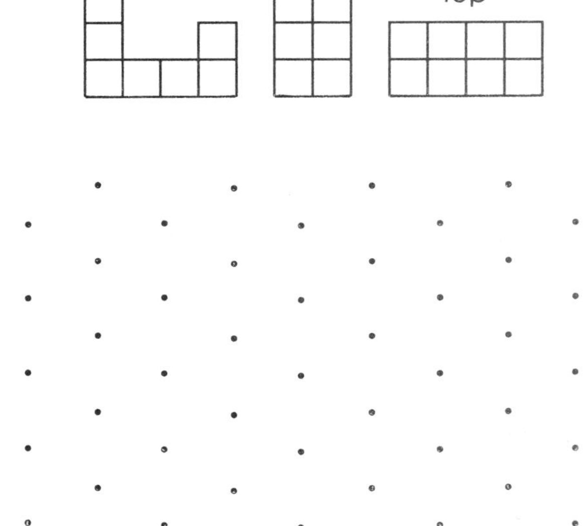

Use a **thermometer** to measure these **temperatures** in **degrees Celsius.**

1. Inside a cupboard ________
2. On a concrete or tiled floor ________
3. At about head height ________
4. Near the ceiling ________
5. Why do we call it the **Celsius** scale?

____

____

____

Show these times on the digital stopwatches in minutes, seconds and hundredths of a second.

6. 5 minutes 10 seconds 3 hundredths

7. 4 minutes 48 seconds 12 hundredths

8. 53 seconds 7 hundredths

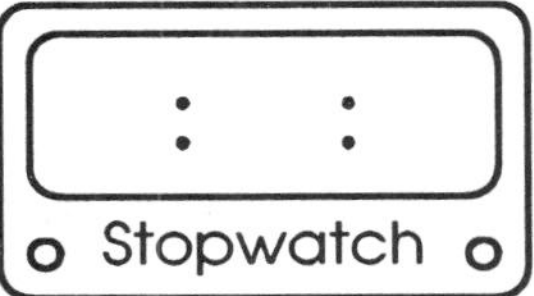

9. 14 minutes 5 seconds

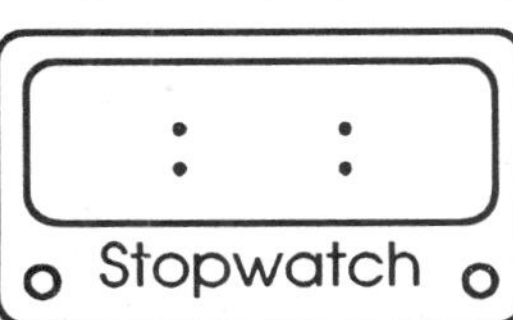

10 How often do we celebreate a:

(a) centenary? ______________

(b) bicentenary? ______________

Write as sums, then work out. The first one is done for you.

11. 6 x 5138 =

```
 5138
  x 6
-----
30828
```

12. 7 x 4490 =

```
  x
-----

-----
```

13. 8 x 3209 =

```
  x
-----

-----
```

14. 7) 430 r

15. 6) 748 r

16. 5) 907 r

17. 9) 682 r

18. 8) 563 r

19. 4) 839 r

Read these stopwatches and write the times in full.

20. 

21.

22.

23. 

________ ________ ________ ________

________ ________ ________ ________

24. 

25. 

26. 

________ ________ ________

________ ________ ________

27. Fill in the gaps.

(a) 1 4 7 10 ____ 16 19 ____

(b) 1 2 4 ____ 16 32 ____ 128

Useful Facts

Time

60 seconds = 1 minute
60 minutes = 1 hour
24 hours = 1 day
7 days = 1 week
14 days = a fortnight
12 months = 1 calendar year
52 weeks = 1 calendar year
365 days = 1 year
366 days = 1 leap year
10 years = a decade
100 years = a century
1 000 years = a millennium

In writing B.C. or A.D. - always place B.C. after the year (536 B.C.); always place A.D. before the year (A.D. 1925).

Angles

acute obtuse right angle

straight reflex

3-D objects

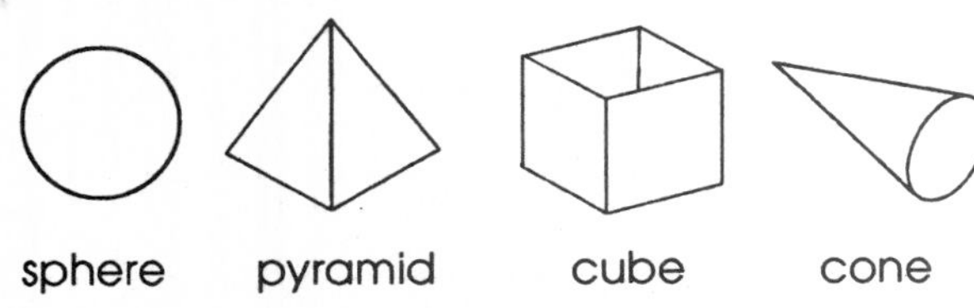

sphere pyramid cube cone

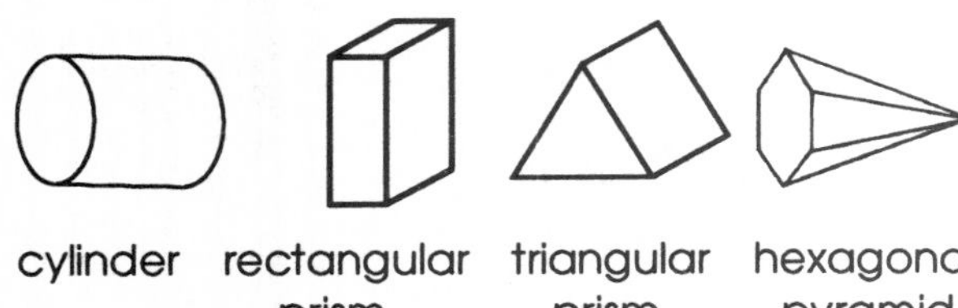

cylinder | rectangular prism | triangular prism | hexagonal pyramid

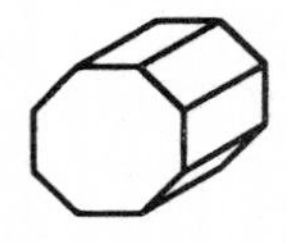

octagonal prism

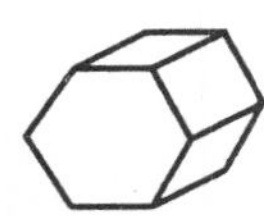

hexagonal prism

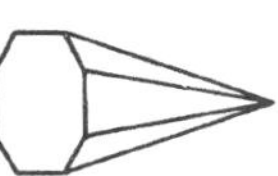

octagonal pyramid

Abbreviations

g = gram(s)
kg = kilogram(s)
ml = millilitre (s)
l = litre(s)
cm = centimetre(s)
m = metre(s)
km = kilometre(s)
mm^2 = square millimetre(s)
cm^2 = square centimetre(s)
m^2 = square metre(s)
ha = hectare(s)
km^2 = square kilometre(s)

Never add s to a metric abbreviation, no matter what the number is.
e.g. 10 cm, 95 cm, 14 km, 83g

Length

10 millimetres = 1 centimetre (cm)
100 centimetres = 1 metre (m)
1 000 metres = 1 kilometre (km)

Capacity

1 000 millilitres (ml) = 1 litre (l)
The weight of 1 millilitre of water is 1 gram
1 000 grams (g) = 1 kilogram (kg)
1 litre of water has a weight of 1 kilogram
1 000 000 cubic centimetres = 1 cubic metre (m^3)

Area

100 square millimetres = 1 cm^2
10 000 square centimetres = 1 m^2
10 000 square metres = 1 hectare (ha)
1 000 000 square metres = 1km^2
100 hectares = 1km^2

Clocks

analog clock

digital clock

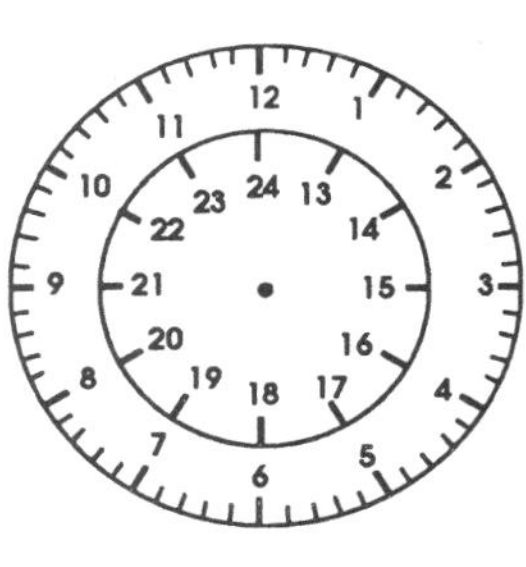

24 hour clock